The Diary of a
Broken Spirit

The Diary of a Broken Spirit

THE SECRETS OF A HOME

JESSICA SEYMOUR

TATE PUBLISHING
AND **ENTERPRISES**, LLC

Published by Tate Publishing & Enterprises, LLC
127 E. Trade Center Terrace | Mustang, Oklahoma 73064 USA
1.888.361.9473 | www.tatepublishing.com

Tate Publishing is committed to excellence in the publishing industry. The company reflects the philosophy established by the founders, based on Psalm 68:11,
"The Lord gave the word and great was the company of those who published it."

Book design copyright © 2016 by Tate Publishing, LLC. All rights reserved.
Cover design by Norlan Balazo
Interior design by Jomar Ouano

Published in the United States of America

ISBN: 978-1-68333-539-9
1. Biography & Autobiography / General
2. Biography & Autobiography / Personal Memoirs
16.04.11

When I was about three years old, my oldest brother used to play this game where he was the doctor and my twin sister and I were the patients. He would make us take all our clothes off and lie on the bed, and then he would make us do sexual favors for him. My sister and I would always fight when it came to playing hide-and-seek because we always knew what would happen as soon as the game started and you were on Robert's team. This went on for years from Texas to Oceanside to North Fork until one day I had had enough. Robert called Jennifer and me outside to go up to his grandma's house because she had ice cream in her freezer. As soon as we got up there, he locked the door behind us and told us that he needed something and that he was wrong about the ice cream. He took off his pants and lay on the bed and told us to come over and give "it" a kiss. Since I had enough, I refused. My sister started to move, and before she started to walk, I grabbed her hand, and then Robert said to come over, or he was going to make us do it. So as he started to make his way over, I grabbed her hand, and we ran for the door. We ran all the way to our house and locked ourselves in the bathroom and stayed until are parents came home.

One time, we were playing hide-and-seek, and I got stuck on Roberts's team, and we were hiding up by my grandma's house out in front. My sister and brother Chris were on the other team, and they were trying to find us. Robert went and sat by this tree and then pulled out his thing and told me to give him a quick blow job, and so I kept putting it off, saying, "I think I hear them" or "Someone is coming." His response was, "Well, hurry before they get here." Then one time when we lived in Texas, the four of us kids were building forts, and Jennifer and Chris were in the boys' room, and Robert and I were in my room. Well, when the fort was done, he told me to take off all my clothes, and he took off his and made me lay facedown on the floor as he climbed on top and had his thing in between my legs and was trying to have sex that way. Then my brother Chris came in and tried to come in the fort, and he saw a little bit of what was going on, but being only two years older than me, he probably didn't understand, and so he just said we were sick and left. This went on for years, and it seemed as though I got the worst of it because my sister was the older one, and so it was the older girl with the younger of the boys.

Then just a few years ago, Jennifer and I were with Robert at my dad's house in San Diego, and my stepsister and the two of us were talking. Somehow we got to agreeing to tell each other something that no one else knew, and I said, "Like, I know something about Robert that could get him into a lot of trouble if anyone found out." Jennifer's eyes got real big, and then Nicole said, "Yeah, well, I know something that could probably get him into more trouble." Then she mentioned that when he lived there, he liked to play this game called doctors and patients, and I said seriously, "That is the same thing I am talking about." Well, my sister never said a word just sat there quietly and listened. Robert always said that if we were to tell anyone that no one would believe us because he is the older brother and that we are just looking for attention, so no one ever spoke a word to anyone. I think about what he did and how he kind of ruined my life—if not the other two's lives as well. When I am next to Eric, Cindy's son, whose mom has been like a second mom to me—or any guy, for that matter—I think about the three years that my brother had ruined my life. It makes me sad and disgusted. It sucks no one should have to deal with that ever. No one knows except Nicole, Jennifer, and my brother Chris.

Chapter 1

Apr. 11, 2001

Well, this kind of is another reason why I have a problem with guys. One night a couple of weeks ago, Jennifer and I were riding the late bus after soccer practice, like we had done for a year now, and this guy named Matt, who lives across the street from us, was sitting next to us up front. Well, our bus driver likes the lights off on the front half of the bus, and I was saying how I had shin splints and how they hurt. Well, he was a helper for the boys' football team and said, "Well, I can help you with them," so he started rubbing my legs. At that point, it didn't bother me, and I should have told him to stop, but I trusted him. I was wearing sweatpants that were about three sizes too big. He kept getting higher and higher on my legs, then he ran his finger across my underwear. I thought that maybe it was an accident, so I did nothing. Then he did it again and again. I moved my legs, and he kept trying. Thankfully it was someone's stop, so I moved my legs completely, and he tried to go down the front of my pants then. That is when I got up and walked away. The rest of the ride, he kept looking at me, and I wouldn't say anything. He then tried to say sorry or something. Then the next day on the bus, he asked me out, but I told him no and then went into what was he thinking, and then he somehow got my number and called me when I got home trying to say sorry and that he didn't know what he was doing, that he really was a nice guy and everything, but I didn't care. I trusted him, and he took advantage of that like everyone does. To add to all this, my mom thinks I am a slut. I mentioned a guy's name, and she comes up with, "You better not get pregnant, or your dad and I will kick your ass." That's all she says. She really doesn't trust that I will try and make good judgments. I wish one day she would say she loves me. I know she does, but she never actually says it.

July 9, 2001

I have had his job for this pick program for about two weeks. Well, my mom and dad went on this trip to Texas to see my stepbrother Cy two weeks ago. Today I woke up for work, and my mom was supposed to take our friend Lilly and her brother's buddy to work because her mom did it when they were gone. I heard my dad yelling, "JoEllen, JoEllen!" I thought they were just fighting again like normal, but to my surprise, my world was going to be turned upside down.

I got this gut feeling that something was wrong, and then I heard him run down the hall to the living room, where my brother was sleeping, and the words that came from his mouth I will never forget. "Son, get up! I think your mother is dead! Call 911."

Then by this time, I had gone into their room. She was lying on the bed. Her eyes were still closed like she was sleeping, so I grabbed her hand, but it was cold. My brother had called 911, and then he handed me the phone. I was trying to listen to the operator, but I was not hearing anything they were saying. It was like a bad dream that I desperately wanted to wake up from. I told the guy on the phone to wait because Jen's dog had heard all the commotion and wanted out of her room. I went in there and said, "Jenn, get up and put your dog out now." Not knowing what was going on, she did, and when she was headed back into her room, which was past my mom's room, she stopped and looked in and saw my mom lying on the floor, me holding the phone, and she just looked really confused and scared.

By this time, my brother was doing CPR on my mom, and my stepdad was in the bathroom throwing up because he had drunk too much the night before, and he just couldn't handle it, I guess. Chris didn't know how to do CPR, so the guy is trying to explain it to me, and I am trying to explain it to my brother. I needed a break, and so I asked my sister to come take over on the phone, and I went and took care of the animals so that when people started showing up, all the dogs were put away. I just needed time to lose it and break down. The firefighters showed up, followed by the ambulance and then the police. Well, they couldn't do anything, so they both left, and the police stayed behind and waited for the coroners. Since the hallway from her bedroom to the living was so small and they had to go out the front door instead of the back door because of space, they asked us all to go outside because it was going to be awkward moving her. By this time, I had remembered that I was supposed to work and asked Jennifer to call Lilly and let her know that we were not going to be able to give her a ride today, so she did. When she got off the phone, I asked if she had told Lilly that we were not going to work and if she could let them know. Jenn said she didn't, so I called Lilly back to tell her.

When I called Lilly back, I asked her if she could let them know we were not going, and she asked, "What's going on? Is everything okay?"

I told her, "I think my mom just died this morning."

I was hoping I was wrong and that they would somehow bring her back. I didn't want to tell Lilly the bad news on the phone, but I could hear in her voice that she was worried. She was my best friend, and she loved my mom like her own. She started crying immediately after I told her. Then a few hours later, she showed up at my house. I guess she went to work and told them, and since she was crying, they told her she could go home if she wanted, and so she came over. When she got there, they had just loaded my mom into the back of the car. My aunt Katie came over, and she was making the calls to the relatives, letting them know what happened, which was nice because I don't think any of us were in the right state to do it. The nightmare started at 5:00 a.m., and the house didn't clear of unwanted people until about 8:30 or nine o'clock.

June 12, 2001

Today, we went to see my mom for the last time. She looked a lot better than the last; they are not sure on what happened yet. After the memorial, we had a get together at the house. Chris had a lot of friends there, and all my relatives were up. By this time, it still really had not hit me yet. I was walking around like nothing was going on, hoping somehow she was going to come walking up. I was waiting for her to pop up at the memorial service, her way of getting everyone together. Her sister Merry didn't show. She probably felt bad because a while back, Merry thought my mom was trying to steal her boyfriend, so they got into a real fist fight and have not spoken since. My aunt is not talking to me because I was headed into my mom's room yesterday and overheard them talking about the things they wanted, like her dolls and some pictures, and, well, I lost it. I yelled and told them they were not taking anything, that it's my mom's things and they were staying were they were and that they all needed to just leave and stay out of her room.

July 17, 2001

Today is the first time that I have ever written this down, but I have been trying to kill myself for years—long before my mom died. Saturday night, I am going to try something new. I am going to take four Robaxin muscle relaxants. Hopefully, this will slow everything down, bringing it to a stop. I have done everything, and I cannot keep doing this. It is not worth it. I just want to see my mom again, to hold her, to kiss her, just to say I love her forever. I miss joking and laughing together.

July 30, 2001

Well, today was kind of weird. I went to work, then soccer practice for three hours. Well, after that at three thirty, I went to the rec center. It closes at five. Matt Williams was looking for his shovel, and so we all jumped into his car to help him find it. Well, after we found it up on the hill, we were going to go back down to the bottom. JJ and I jumped on the hood of the car while my sister sat inside. Everything was going okay, and I don't know what he was thinking, but Matt decided to go faster. Well, I guess he didn't see the tree in front of him because we were blocking his view, so I yelled, "Matt, there is a tree," and he didn't turn, so I yelled again, and then JJ and I looked at each other and jumped, and Matt hit the tree dead on. We got up and looked at where we were sitting. Our legs would have been pinned, and we would have flown up into the tree and then back down on the car. Matt is such an idiot. Then he wanted to get something from the store, so we went with him. He was pulling out of the gas station, and instead of using the driveway, he went right off the curb and ended up punching a hole in his oil tank. Oil was leaking everywhere, and it messed up his car. School starts in three weeks. It would be my sophomore year, but I don't want to go.

Sept. 1, 2001

Well, I just got my last paycheck. I would have loved to spend some of it on my mom, but she died two weeks into my job. I have decided that I don't want to kill myself anymore. I just want things to be like they used to be. My mom would still be alive, my old friends would still talk to me, Lilly wouldn't be in love with my brother, and I would have someone to hug. I would tell them I love them, and they would tell that they would be there for me no matter what. Scott Gayton still liked me, and everything would finally be all right. I know that would never happen, but it really hurts when I think about all of it. One day, someone is going to read this and think I am really stupid or something.

Aug. 4, 2001

In two weeks, we finally start school again. The only difference is I won't be able to come home and tell my mom all about it. My mom's death was the greatest shock to me. I then realized how hard it was to keep this house clean. There are 4 kids, and no matter what, this house is always dirty. I miss my mom so much. And then we have Cindy Swarts, a really close friend of the family. She is like a second mom to us kids. She is always there when we need to talk or want a hug. I am so glad we have her, and I don't know what would happen if I lost her too.

Nov. 22, 2001

Today is the first time we will be going to my aunt's and grandma's house without my mom. We are going to celebrate Thanksgiving, something we have never done before. We usually stay home and go around Christmastime, but we are not going back down later. We are visiting all my mom's side of the family, and it's kind of nice because my mom liked to start Christmas shopping early, and so she had bought things for her side of the family already, and they sit in a box and wait till Christmas when she wraps it all and hands it out. By the way, I have failed to write about my dad's new girlfriend. Her name is Pam, and to me, it is too soon to already be bringing her home. The first day he brought her home, it was late, and you can tell they both had been drinking because they woke the whole house up trying to walk. Then they began to have sex, and she is so loud that faking or not, I was super upset. I had to get up early and go to school, and you can just hear them moaning and screaming, so after a few minutes, I just got tired of it and turned my radio on loud enough to drown out the noise. No courtesy around here, I swear. Pam doesn't want Dad to go because she thinks he wouldn't want to come back to her after spending a week with Mom's family. I think this trip will be good for all of us.

Nov. 19, 2001

Yesterday, my late bus driver was arrested. He was charged with sexually assaulting a kid. No one knows who the kid was who claimed it, and there is no information to go off of. I don't believe he would have done anything like that, and it was probably a boy who wanted attention. He loves his job way too much to even consider thinking about it. His name is Shawn. I hope all charges against him are dropped and that he returns back to our school and keeps his job. He is a very nice man. I know more about him than I do my real dad, and I know he didn't do it, so I wish him luck.

Dec. 3, 2001

We had our second soccer game today, and the latest on Shawn is that he is charged with misdemeanors, but he will never work for Sierra again. I would be much happier if I got to see him and if he came back, driving our bus like normal. Well, the game was 2–1. We won. Every country song makes me think of Shawn and all the fun we had on the bus after school for the last two years.

Dec. 4, 2001

Well, I found out today that Shawn was fired, so he won't be coming back. I think I am going to get his address and write him. Well, today I got a new puppy from my uncle. She already has a name, and it is Rally. Tomorrow we have a game, so I hope we do well. Well, I think someone read this because it was in the wrong spot. Oh well, it will be in a big safe very soon, so I can't wait. I miss Cindy. I have not seen her in six days. I won't be seeing a lot of her because are games are on different days.

Dec. 13, 2001

Well, I have not written for a couple of days. I have the worst luck with guys. My brother had this party, and, well, this guy wouldn't leave me alone until I gave him a kiss, so I did so he would leave. Then he goes to school thinking he is a big shot. Well, his name is Gunnar. He then called me up and asked me out. Well, of course I told him no. His friend Nick likes me, and he is trying to flirt, but he is making it very obvious. Well, the latest on Shawn is that they don't think he did it anymore, but he still can't work for the district because that will be on his record. My soccer coach Careen lost her grandpa, so she wasn't at school, and we have a tournament tomorrow. I wish her luck with her life, and I know how it feels to lose someone that means something to you.

Dec. 17, 2001

For the last couple of nights, I have cried for like an hour and a half, and every time I do, my sister claims something happens to her in her room. Well, if it's my mom, that would be so cool, even if I got to see her for, like, ten minutes. That might cheer me up a little. I have been so depressed, and I am trying to keep myself busy because I didn't seem so mad all the time. I miss my mom a lot. It makes me sad, and I want to cry when I think about her. There is really no one I can talk to because no one feels the same way, maybe Kelley would, but I don't know how I would bring it up. Then there is Cindy, but I am afraid I would just drive her away. I hardly see her anymore anyways, so it wouldn't change anything. If I got professional help, it probably wouldn't work because I am so freaking shy. It sucks. I wish I could just speak my mind without getting mad and red in the face and sweating. I found out that if I write my feelings down, it helps me out. I don't feels so bad. It is like taking a load off. I wish someone knew how I felt, and they would help me out. They would talk to me, help me understand my problems and not judge me. My mom is so beautiful. I wish I could tell her that and that I love her one more time and that I have thought about her every day since she passed away.

Dec. 21, 2001

It is so close to Christmas, spending it without my mom will be hard. On the twenty-second, I was cleaning my grandma's house, and my friend Savannah Ward showed up and brought Jenny Jen and me a Christmas present. My dad and I have been drifting apart since he got his new girlfriend. He smokes weed and drinks a lot more now, and everyone is worried about us kids. I wish I lived with someone else. On the twenty-third, my friend Kelley brought over cheesecake, and she went down the wrong driveway and got stuck. Then we walked all the way to my house, and Jenn and I took our red car to try and pull her out, which didn't work, so then the neighbor Edd came by and, with his truck, pulled her out. It was kind of funny, but she was all worried because it was her dad's car.

Dec. 26, 2001

Christmas came and went. It was funny. It seemed like a regular day; it didn't make me excited or depressed. The few gifts sat on the table. We went found out which ones were ours and opened them, thanked everyone, and watched TV. The thing I really liked was my safe because I can lock all my items in it that I don't want read or stolen. I found out that I write a lot of stuff down that I really don't mean, which is quiet funny if anyone actually read this. That is in case anybody reads this. They would know that they are wasting their time.

Dec. 28, 2001

Well, I have not seen my dad for three days. Like now, he is home, but has been up in the shed for the past six hours. I think he wasn't home when we got here at twelve, then he showed up sometime later. He has Pam come down and get him everything, like food or a beer. Who cares, though. I worry enough about myself and about who is going to do the grocery shopping so I can cook us kids dinner. It doesn't really faze me. I am going to see how long I can go without saying anything to him.

Chapter 2

Jan. 19, 2002

They finally found out what happened to my mom after several months. She had a probable cardiac problem due to myocardial hypertrophy, which means she had an enlarged heart because she had high blood pressure, and it got too big that one day it just stopped working. I no longer start for out soccer team, and I hardly play anymore. I don't know why I just don't feel motivated to do anything.

Mar. 1, 2002

My dad has had the life insurance money for about a week. He has not told us, but you can tell. He went out and bought a thousand-dollar refrigerator and a new TV, which we don't need either. Then he went and bought a new tractor. He is spending money left and right. I asked for one thing—a down payment on a car—and I would work off the rest. He got over $104,936.72 dollars, and it is almost gone. He says it will be gone very soon because he is paying all the bills off. If he got me a car, I would love it because it would be like the last gift from my mom. I miss her more and more each day.

Mar. 28, 2002

Today I got my permit, and Jenn and I stayed up till 1:48 a.m. Well, she was tired, so she asked if she could sleep in my room again, I said yes, but not Cookie, her dog. She got mad and said, "I hope whenever you get an animal that they all die." It was pretty mean, and I tried to be nice. She just always cuts me down. She makes me hate myself because I never say the right words or do the right thing. I am so clueless and dumb. I hate it so much.

Mar. 29, 2002

Well, Jenn and I went to the movies. On the way home, I was wearing my new shorts, and I bled all over them. Well, it would not be that bad, but my dad and his girlfriend saw it. I am so embarrassed, and it sucks. Well, I think there is something wrong with my insides because I get really sharp pains in my stomach, and my periods go on forever, and I bleed way too much. I wish I could just die. I am so tired of living and going through all these problems on my way home. Jen and I were kind of joking around, and he thought we were fighting. He gets really upset and turns around, grabs my arm, and goes into the other lane, and then he has to swerve out of the way of an oncoming car. He keeps yelling and turning around and keeps running off the road. He is going to kill us one day out of madness. One minute, he is yelling, and the next, he is saying sorry.

Mar. 30, 2002

Today, my dad and his girlfriend are cleaning my mom's stuff out. They're taking her clothes and giving them to Goodwill. They took most of her dolls and threw them in the shed. I can somewhat understand him picking stuff up, but he doesn't need to give it all away. The thing is, he did it while we were at school. Was he hoping that he could get it all done before we got home or what? I can't stand it. I do not want to live here anymore. He makes me sick. He is an alcoholic and a pot smoker. He tries to make up after a fight over nothing when he was wrong.

Apr. 8, 2002

Today I found out that Scott Gayton can lie right to your face and you would not even know it. Well, a lady who works at our school got killed yesterday. What happened was her husband shot her and then killed himself. They had five girls. My friend's uncle was drunk and walked in the middle of the road. Well, a car hit him, and he was dead on the spot. Pam is going to move in with us. It won't be bad because she will be saving money, I guess. She has been living with her daughter because she had a nervous breakdown after her husband killed himself. This also means that if they split, she won't have anywhere to go, but if they get married again, it would be his third wife and her second husband. His first wife cheated on him and got pregnant by a different man, his second wife died, and her first husband killed himself. I will be living with people who are not blood, but I guess that is how foster children do it.

May 10, 2002

For the past three days, I have been getting really bad headaches, and then I will get really sharp pains in my stomach. It comes back again. It wishes it would stay gone. I can't handle it. I think I need to go to the doctor's. My dad only thinks of himself. He has his problems, but, well, what about mine? I hope I can just pass out from the pain, then I will have to go to the doctor's. There would be no choice. They will do tests and find out what is wrong, if anything. I really like Scott Gayton. Still, I don't know why we don't go out. I think we will make a cute couple, but these headaches make me become a different person that no one wants to be around. They make me so angry. I yell at everyone for nothing, then I feel really bad when they go away. I hope it will go away or gets fixed. If I know what it is, I can treat it, but I need to find out why I'm getting them first.

May 18, 2002

Fifteen days left of school. I can't wait. If there was anything that I could get, I would get my mom back. I would take my life to spare hers, and then at least I can look down upon her. Anyways I applied for a job and found out my stepdad quit his. How are we supposed to live? He is not working, and he has his girlfriend, so I asked him if she is supposed to support him and the two of us. Well, he told Jenn and me to get a job so he wouldn't have to pay for our school clothes or anything. Well, what happens when the money runs out? I can't have a job, go to school, and play soccer. I will probably have to quit soccer because my grades come first. I am getting as far away as possible. I wish it was like old times. I miss it.

May 23, 2002

Rally had her puppies today. They're so cute. She had eight total. There are only two that look a little like her. All the rest are white and yellow. She is black and brown and a little white. Well, there is a pure black one, then there is a black-and-gray one. She only had two girls, and they're both white. Well, I don't want to get rid of them, but I know I am going to have to. Dad didn't want her to be pregnant in the first place, but since I had to pay to get her fixed and I didn't have the money, I had to wait.

July 8, 2002

Leoma and her family had a memorial service for her dad. He was eighty-six years old, and he died on June 30. It brought back a lot of memories, and seeing Leoma so sad made me want to cry because I know how she feels, and there is nothing you can do to forget about it or get over it. Well, she said it meant a lot to her that we were there, and it really does. It shows you that people really care about you.

July 9, 2002

Today is one year since my mom died, and Cindy Swarts took us out to dinner since my dad went camping. It was a lot of fun. We laughed and joked about all kinds of things. It was all of us kids and Chris's girlfriend, which was nice. Cindy and Mark seem so happy together. It makes me wonder why parents fight so much and why my parents seemed like they hated each other so very much.

July 20, 2002

Today, I went to our workshop like every Friday. Then Jenn, JJ, and I all went to the rec center. Well, our soccer coach said we needed to run some, so we went to the school. JJ was having a party, so after that, we went to his house took a shower. We drove to my house to get some beer money, but we needed someone to buy it for us. We then went to Lilly's house. Lafe had Nathen Hodges buy the beer for us. We stayed and partied at Lilly's house instead. Lilly's mom was giving me a shot of tequila. I was drinking beer and tequila. I guess I drank too much because I don't remember that night, but everyone says I was throwing up for a good four hours and that someone was going to take me to the hospital. Well, supposedly before that happened, I guess JJ and I had sex in front of everyone in Lilly's room on her floor. Then we moved to the bathroom, where we did it again. I can't believe no one had the brains to tell either one of us not to do it. What I hear is he was pretty drunk too. The thing that keeps running through my mind was if he was wearing a condom or not. I don't think he was for the simple fact that, well, where would he have gotten one? Jenn said she had a dream that I was pregnant and that I had a little girl. I am not ready for this. I would be killed just for having sex. Could you imagine what would happen? Not to mention that I guess we dropped Jenn off, and then went I went to JJ's house that night. The next morning, I was sleeping, and the alarm went off because I had to be home before his mom got there. He opened the blinds, and I was still kind of drunk, and he climbed on top of me again, and we did it again. Then he dropped me off, and I went back to sleep for a few hours.

Aug. 5, 2002

Today was the last day of work. All our supervisors took us all out to pizza. It was fun. Mark Stomas hates to be in public, so he didn't really want to go, but we finally talked him into going. It was so much fun. We were making jokes about everything. Well, last night, Stacy called looking for my brother and asked if I was pregnant. She told me that JJ had said I was pregnant with his kid about two weeks ago. I asked him about it. He said he didn't say anything. But that her brother might be mad because JJ took his smokes and that might be the only way he had a chance to get back at him. Well, Cindy has been back for about a week now, and she's told JJ she had a present for us. I haven't seen her for a while. My grandma and aunt are supposed to be up in a few days to take Jenn and me school shopping. School starts soon. I would have liked a week off from work before school starts up again. I still have a second book to read for language class. Don't know why I signed up for honors English. LOL.

Aug. 11, 2002

Well, I still have not had my period yet, maybe because I am so stressed. I don't know what I would do if I was pregnant. I would be such a disgrace to my family, to God, to my friends, and to myself. I can't even take care of myself, let alone a child. My dad thinks I am the perfect one, that Jenn is the one who needs to be watched. If I got pregnant, he would disown me like everyone else. I can't believe I let something like this happen. I am so stupid.

Aug. 17, 2002

Well, yesterday I had a sign of my period and was so happy when I woke up today. There is no way I could be pregnant. Now I am so thankful that I didn't have to go through the trouble I don't think I could handle it. Well, Savannah's birthday party was a lot of fun. It was yesterday. It was at the lake. I went all around the lake with Jake Wright on the tube and Jet Ski. Well, Scott Gayton's surprise party is tomorrow. He will be turning sixteen. School starts on Monday.

Aug. 27, 2002

Today I was talking to Scott on the phone. He is thinking about hooking up with a senior named Jenni. I told him I wanted to go to the formal, and he said, "This year, you and I are going."

I said, "Cool, with whom?"

He then said, "With each other."

So then I said it wouldn't happen if he was going to get a girlfriend. He said that it wouldn't matter, that nothing will change it. Yeah, right! It would be cool, though, if we went together. He said this girl Jenni reminds him of me, that she is just like me, but, of course, she is prettier. To him, that is what matters most…Oh well.

My brother was just joking and said I was pregnant and that I probably had AIDS from JJ. He is playing. JJ told everyone about what had happened. I don't know if I mentioned it already. Well, Travis Windmiller, Nick, and Will Elis know. JJ told them all the details and everything. I don't know why he is so proud. I regret every minute of it. It was horrible. I don't remember it, and he is telling everyone everything that happened like they need to know. People are coming up to me asking if it is true or not, and I don't know what they're talking about. Well, Travis spelled to Jenn what had happened in the morning at JJ's house, and she got mad and called me a slut. Travis got mad at JJ because he is telling everyone about it, and he shouldn't. Travis has a little crush on me, but I don't want to date him, especially now that he knows I had sex with JJ.

Sept. 8, 2002

Yesterday we had a soccer game. We tied 0–0. It was hard but still fun. Well, Jenn got kicked out again over something so stupid, so she is at Lilly's house. It was ridiculous. I have not even seen the fat drunk since I left yesterday. I hate him. He is so unreasonable and difficult to talk to. He gets so mad over nothing. It is stupid. Well, I am not pregnant. There is no way I could be, so it's great. I am happy for that. I'm glad I get one more chance. Not many people get one.

Sept. 20, 2002

I missed my period. I looked it up, and it says it could because of several things, like hormones are different and things like that. I am really scared because there is a girl, who is out playing soccer. Rumor has it she has a cyst, and she really looks pregnant. Her stomach is big and really tight. I don't want to go through that. Well, I am going to order a test to make sure. I don't know what I will do if I was. I will probably try to kill myself or something. My life is going good right now. I am getting along with my dad and everything. I really don't want this to hurt our friendship. Everyone will think I am a slut. It will really ruin my life. I have decided that I am going to quit drinking until I get out of high school and I know what I am going to do. I still can't believe I actually did that. I am so stupid. Alcohol makes you do some really stupid things. I hate myself for it.

Chapter 3

I have not written in a long time, so here it goes. January 1, 2003, our stepdad kicked us out, (Jenn and I) because we wanted our social security money and Jenn's dog was on his bed. Well, we moved in with Tom and Janet. I was still getting really bad pains in my stomach. I got one of my pains in front of Janet one night. She got scared and the next day took me to the doctors. She wanted to take me to Fresno to the emergency room, but I didn't really want to go, so I told her, "I will go in the morning. That way, we can get into Oakhurst." Well, good news! I no longer have to worry about being pregnant. See, that visit led to more, well. On the first one, they thought my muscles were contracting. Then they said it was my ovulation period (yeah right). They gave me these little green pills that would knock me on my butt. Then finally they think I have endometriosis, so they put me on birth control pills to see if the pain will go away. Well, tomorrow we were all leaving to go to Hawaii for eight days to celebrate our birthdays. Jen and I got a 2002 silver Pontiac Sunfire as an early birthday present. We are getting are social security money now. I love where I am living. My whole life has changed for the better. I am finally happy and stress free. I'm getting good grades and saving money, and I finally have an answer to some of my pains.

May 1, 2003

Well, today we got back from Hawaii (Maui). It was so fun. On our birthday, we went out to eat, and we went snorkeling in the ocean. I got Scott Gayton the sand he wanted and a shell necklace. I got Kelley and Melanie a glass thing. I had so much fun. Well, we opened an account, and so far, I have $989.77 in it. My real dad just sent me $50 for my birthday. I didn't think he was going to be sending us any more money. After Mom died, he wanted us to move down there, but we didn't want to because of our friends and school, so he told us he was going to stop the child support because we probably wouldn't get it anyways. So I am going to put it in my bank. Well, my birth control pills are working. I got the pains a little, but not nearly as bad. The bad thing about it is I was on my period almost the whole time in Hawaii, but I still had so much fun. Well, Jenn is talking to our dad right now, so I got to go and thank him for the birthday money.

May 11, 2003

Yesterday was the junior-senior prom for our school. Well, Jenn went with her boyfriend Keegan Childers, and I went with Scott Gayton. On the way down to Fresno, we got into a car accident. There was a black truck, and the guy driving it turned into his driveway and didn't bother using his turn signal. Well, the white car behind him came to a complete stop fast, so we slammed on our brakes. We were pretty close, and we were all thankful we didn't hit them. Well, this white truck behind us was going really fast and not paying attention and rear-ended us, pushing us into the white car. We still made it to the prom, but we were late. My neck was hurting so bad.

Well, we all cooked dinner tonight, and Scott was invited, but he went out with his mom. I wish we could go out.

May 19–20, 2003

On the nineteenth, Jennifer got a ride home from Keegan, and they went to Oakhurst first. Well, I got home and told Tom where she was. Amanda jumps in and says, "Well, you should ground her and everything."

So Jenn gets home, and Tom says, "Where were you?"

She says, "I went to Oakhurst."

He goes, "Well, did you ask?"

She said, "I told Jess to tell you," and he goes, "That is not asking."

Amanda says, "Well, that isn't good enough."

She is grounded for a week. The next day, I went out to the car to go to the bus stop, and the doors are locked. Both sets of keys are in the car. I think Amanda did it because she was the last one outside and you have to lock both doors by hand. She likes being the center of attention and getting people in trouble. I saw JJ today. I was in the car, and he was walking. He recognized me, but I acted like I didn't see him.

July 22, 2003

On the twentieth, Jenn and I went to Kegan's aunt's house for dinner. Well, Jen and I went back to Kegan's, and he went to pick up Will Elis. We both lay on the couch to watch a movie that we rented. It was really fun. I think I am starting to like him. We have spent a lot of time together because he is Kegan's best friend and Jennifer is dating Keegan, so it seems like the four of us are always together. Today, Jenn and I went back over there, and he acted as if he was sleeping, so I started flirting with him and stuff. I like him. I don't know if he actually likes me or if he is just playing for fun and really doesn't care. Well, he is the type that I wouldn't think would actually flirt like we do, but he does, and I don't want him to stop. I would love it if he asked me out. It would be cool, and he probably would grow out of his shyness.

Aug. 10, 2003

Today Renee and I were talking. I feel so bad for her. She has had it bad. When she was fourteen, Tom had slept with her. She hates him with a passion. She says he did it to a ton of girls, and I was just thinking how that would mess someone up. Anyways, she told me to mention her name and see what he does. Well, I told him that Renee knows him, and he says, "Don't you know by now that everyone knows me and I just forget who they are?" Well, I know something happened by how upset she gets when his name is being mentioned. I wish there was something more I could do. She wants to go to sleep one night and just not wake up. I hope she realizes that I love her like a mother and that I'm thankful she has been there for me.

Sept. 9, 2003

Well, Tom kicked us out, saying we didn't treat him like a parent. I told him we give him respect, and he says we worked too much and that we can live off his money and that he will support us. He said we could only live with our real dad, our foster care, that we can't stay in North Fork, that we were not welcome. Well, our dad was on his way to pick us up, and Tom called our work and told them we had to quit and everything. He took away our car, which we paid for, took our cell phone, and said if we can't obey his rules, we shouldn't be able to live in North Fork with our friends, go to the same school, and all that stuff, like he owns the whole town. Our dad called and talked to Cindy for a while, and she changed his mind, so we got to stay. We finished our job, and I am happy. My dad said the reason why he is letting us stay with Cindy is because the only time he has ever seen my brother Chris truly happy is when he was living with her. He also said he never liked Tom and didn't like the way he talked to us.

Sept. 21, 2003

We had a going-away party for Brandon because he was going into the army. There was a lot of drinking. Jason just got home from Iraq. He is in the military, and he was really drunk. Well, he was outside, and I went out there to talk to him, and he leaned over and gave me a kiss. Well anyway, that night, I was sleeping on the couch, and he came out looking for me. He asked me to follow him back into the bedroom. I did. We started making out, and the thing Travis always tells me kept running through my head, how I always play and then leave them hanging, so I followed through, and we had sex. Well, I asked if he had a condom, and he said no. He said he uses the pull-out method and that it works, and I believed him. I hadn't had my period yet, but it could be because of the entire street I went through. Let's hope. He is nineteen.

Oct. 11, 2003

Well, Eric and I have been fooling around since I moved in. We had some drinks at a wedding, and, well, we kind of played on the way home. He said how he wants me really bad and that he can't have me. Well, yeah, we ended up having sex, but what is cool about it is he understands that I don't know what I am doing, and he seems like he cares, but I don't know if he really likes me or if I am his girl on the side. I think he either has a girlfriend or he is trying to get one. I really don't know if he likes me or if he was just drunk and just really wanted some. I did make him use a condom, and he did not seem to care about it, and he seems to care about my needs. I like him, but I am not sure if he feels the same way. He is older than I am. He is twenty-two, and I am seventeen, so we will have to keep it a secret. I am not sure if it's because of the age difference, me living with his parents, or if he has someone else.

Oct. 17, 2003

Well, today Eric and I slept together again. Jenn and Travis took Steve home, and Cindy and Mark went to bed. We were sitting on the couch, and he asked me if I would give him a blow job. I was afraid we would get caught, so he moved all the way to the end of the couch, and I acted as if I was lying in his lap. Jen and Travis came home, and he put the pillow there to cover up his hard-on. I still don't know if he likes me or if he is just playing. I think he does, but I can't be 100 percent sure. Everyone I hang out with is always calling me names and making fun of me because of him. They call me a slut and all this stuff. Well, I try to ignore them. I am finally starting to trust guys again, and hopefully I start my period in two weeks.

Oct. 21, 2003

Today I gave blood. It wasn't bad. I got to thinking about me possibly being pregnant, and I felt horrible. Eric asked me if I would come visit him tonight, and I got to thinking how the guys are probably right about me being a used-up girl, who just tries to find any man that can please me. Anyways, I don't think I will go see him. He is nice, but I really don't know how he feels about me.

Oct. 31, 2003

Well, today is Mark's birthday, and Eric is still out fighting the fires since he works for the forestry department, putting the fires out. He should be home next week. I still have not had my period. I am kind of hoping it is because I started soccer, which can lead to me being late. I am trying to see if I gained weight or not. Travis doesn't like me anymore, and I really want a boyfriend, but I don't know what I really want. I always find myself thinking about everything I have dealt with, and I know there are people who are way worse off. It's just that I am trying, but I don't know what for. My family will think I am just a big mistake, especially if I was pregnant. It would make my mom so disappointed in me. I can feel her looking down on me. Sometimes I pray to be better and try not to disappoint her, but sometimes I can't help it. I don't know why I do it. I just get into the situation, and I don't say no. I let it continue, or I do, and they say something, and I know it is wrong, but I just continue to do it. I hope my wish comes true, that I am not pregnant, and I hope someone will end it for me for good so I can see my mom and not get myself in these situations anymore. I am retarded.

Nov. 7, 2003

I still haven't had my period. I called it off with Eric last week. I think he is talking to this girl on the Internet and plans on meeting her. Anyways, soccer tryouts were posted today, and I made the varsity team again. I think I am going to buy a test someday. I don't know how or when. I don't know what I would do if I was to find out I am pregnant. It would be the death of me. I would tell Jason, somehow, but I would also have a plan on what to do to end my life. Eric and I always used a condom, and I was taking my pill regularly. I can't believe I let myself do that with Jason. I am so stupid to let myself go like that. I really think I am through because I am like a week or two late. I am so stupid. Just as everything is going well, I find a reason to screw it up.

Nov. 10, 2003

Jenn and I went down to Fresno to the mall and took pictures together. They came out really well. We were supposed to take ten poses and pick seven, then decide the sizes. Well, we took fifteen poses, picked our seven, and then I bought the rest of the proofs. It was fun. I guess it cost $58 and then $15 for the extra proofs if we wanted them, so I bought them.

Nov. 15, 2003

Today Jen and I went back down to Fresno to pick up our 6×10 pictures from last week. Well, on the way down, I told Jen I wanted to buy a test to know if I was pregnant or not. We got to the mall, and they have Longs drug store in there, so Jenn and I went and found the test. Well, I didn't want to buy it, but I needed it. Jenn picked it up and put it on the counter. Well, she wanted to make sure the man at the counter knew it wasn't for her, so she is like, "Jess, you going to buy anything else?" The guy started laughing. Finally I paid for it. We picked up our pictures and then went home. Well, the first thing I do is take the test to the bathroom and read the directions. I took the test, and thank God it was negative. Later, I am sitting at the computer thinking if I should maybe do it again to make sure, but if I did everything right the first time, it should be correct. Well, about this time, someone knocks at the door, and it was Jason. He was in his uniform. He looked hot. Well anyway, I was thinking how I would have told him he was going to be a dad just hours before. Anyways, after he was here for a while, I kind of started my period, then I took my pill, so it went away. Then he left to change and came back. Everyone had gone to sleep, and it was just him and me. He told me he remembered last time. We made out for a while, and he asked me if I wanted to do it. I told him no. Just thinking about the day I had and the promise I had made. Well, he told me that he has to go back to Iraq, so then I felt bad, but I couldn't do it, so instead we lay there. He kept asking me, and I said no. He got off anyways, but we didn't have sex. He goes back in February.

Dec. 7, 2003

Last night was close. Jason and Eric showed up at 1:00 a.m., and they came into the room, and so Jenn and I went to watch *Super Troopers*. Well, Eric went to sleep. So did Jenn. It was just Jason and me in the living room. Well, we lay next to each other for a while. We started making out, but then he slid off the couch, and I didn't know why. A second later, Cindy was standing there. She started asking me questions, and Jason acted as if he were asleep. He must have heard her because it was perfect timing. It was a very close call. I went to bed, she stayed up, and Jason just lay on the floor. Then since everyone had to work in the morning, the house was empty. Jason was still there, and so before he left, we had sex, and this time, I did not worry because I got back on the pill, and so I can't get pregnant.

Dec. 22, 2003

Well, today I found out that Bernadet is coming up to visit. That is Eric's online girlfriend. I don't know how long she is staying or if the two are actually serious. Travis and Steve were over, and they were making fun of me because of it. Steve said Cindy and Mark had to know just by the way I act around him. I don't think they do, or at least they haven't said anything about it.

Dec. 31, 2003

On New Year's Eve, Cindy and everyone went out and gave Jen and me permission to invite friends over but said no drinking. Well, Scott Gayton, Travis Windmiller, Steve Cook, Jake Wright, and Melanie Harris were all over, and, of course, we were drinking. Scott, who I have liked for a long time, had to be home at midnight, and so I got ready to take him. It was eleven. Everyone asked why we had wanted to leave so early. He said he wanted to drive slowly, so I said, "Okay, let's go. Whatever, I don't care."

Well, we turned down the road toward his house. He said, "Slow down and turn left up here," so I did, knowing he lives on the right. We ended up fooling around, but it was extremely difficult in the car. Then I took him home, dropped him off, went back to mine. Everyone had to have known because he called before I got back. Then everyone was making fun of me all night.

Chapter 4

Jan. 8, 2004

Today we just got all our graduation stuff, and I got to thinking that school is almost over and that I am going to be out and that I am going to miss everyone. What I am going to do? Oh well, got to grow up someday and get out in the real world.

Jan. 13, 2004

Last night, I found out that Eric broke up with his girlfriend. Well, we ended up having sex, so in order for me to keep my new year's revolution, I can't sleep with anyone but him. According to Travis, I can't sleep with or do anything with any guy unless I have gone out with him for at least a month. So I broke that one because we are not going out. I didn't tell Jenn because I don't want her to tell the guys.

Jan. 18, 2004

I think it is really over with Eric. He doesn't do anything he used to. I should move on because I am just hurting myself prancing around, trying to get him to notice me. He doesn't like me, but I am still waiting. I really like Eric, but I am too chicken to tell him. I believe he doesn't feel the same way. Everyone is trying to get me to go out with Steve. He is a nice guy. I just think he is too nice. I don't know what I should do about Steve. I have no reason not to like him. I will have to think about it.

Feb. 14, 2004

Jenn and I went to Fresno to watch a movie, we saw *50 First Dates*. Anyways, Steve, Travis, and Jake wanted us to come over and watch movies. Well, I knew this was my opportunity with Eric because Jenn wouldn't be around. I figured she would go by herself. Well, she finally went, then Cindy and Mark went to bed early. Eric came out of his room and walked over to where I was sitting, trying not to act like he was trying to get my attention. He asked if I wanted to kiss him because he was getting sick, and trust me, I didn't turn him down. He asked me a couple of questions like if I got a boyfriend, would we stop what we were doing. I told him I don't know, that it would depend on how I feel about the person. Then he asked if I would miss him if he moved out. I told him yes. Every time we're together, I am like a different person. He asked if he was the first person I had given a blow job to. Of course he was. The other stuff was forced, so it doesn't count. Anyways, I have changed a lot, like before I wouldn't do anything with the lights on, but now I give him head in the living room, with both parents up in their room, and we fuck with the lights on. We talk. I know he talks to other girls on the phone, but he has not met them. He said I almost had the perfect body. I just need a little more ass. He also said I gave head like a pro, which is always good to hear. At least I know I won't disappoint any guy I plan to fool around with.

Feb. 18, 2004

I don't know why I waste my time on Eric. When everyone goes to bed, I stay up hoping he would come out and take me away. I act like I am getting water so that maybe he will open his door. I wait for him all the time when I could be flirting with other guys, but I end up dreaming about him, trying to look nice for him. He is always who I talk about and think about. He is always on my mind.

Feb. 19, 2004

Last night was very interesting. You know how I always say I will try anything once. Well, we were at Jacob's house with beer. It's his girlfriend Katie, me, him, in his room. She says, "You want to make out to see what the guys will do?"

Anyways, the idea faded, and then Jacob is talking about his package. Katie then says, "You want to have a threesome?" He gets embarrassed. I told them I needed a few more beers. Later, Katie and I started making out. Well, we were trying to get Jake hard, and it wasn't working. I don't know about you, but if I were a guy, and my dream was having a threesome, it wouldn't take me that long to pop a boner. Well, the plan was go for five minutes to see what everyone would say. Well, Jake couldn't do it. Katie and I are laying butt naked on his bed, making out, but he couldn't get halfway. We tried everything. She gave him head, then I tried. We tried hand jobs—everything. We had him watch us. It didn't work, then Katie and I jumped in the shower. He still wanted to try, so he got in as well. By this time, we had an audience—Gunnar, who was also there goes in the bathroom and sits on the toilet lid and says he has to pee. Steve is standing in the doorway. Amanda stayed in the living room with Jen and Travis. Everyone knew Jacob couldn't get it up. He ran down the hall naked, yelling he needed Viagra. So it didn't work out. We went back into the room and continued. He finally got it up, and Katie got mad and smacked him.

Feb. 20, 2004

Last night, we tied Steve up at Jake's house and pulled his pants down to his ankles. We then tied him to a metal chair and took off his shirt. We put makeup on him, put a banana and two oranges in his pants, and then we took pictures. He wasn't mad, and he really didn't care. Tonight we are going to do it to Travis.

Feb. 22, 2004

Eric and I have been flirting like crazy since he got home. He is turning me on.

Feb. 23, 2004

Last night, we had sex. Well, today at school, Jean told everyone about what happened. She keeps calling me Bi. Everyone was making fun of me because of Eric. Jen and all the guys said I am going to get kicked out because I am stupid and I can't hold off. They said I am fucking with Cindy's trust and that she would be so pissed off if she found out.

Feb. 29, 2004

Yesterday we went to Oakhurst to put job applications in. Well, when we got into our car, Jenn turned it on, and steam was coming up from the manifold. We come to find out that we might have blown a head gasket or cracked it.

Well, Mel, Jen, and I were going to a party, and Eric asked what time I would be home. I told him I didn't know. He said he would wait up for me. Mel fooled around with Gunnar, and Jen kissed Travis. We got home at twelve thirty. Eric was already asleep, so Jen writes him, "R you up?" He then turned his light on, so I went over. I told him Jenn knew and that she was the one who wrote the message. My hands were shaking. I was so nervous. Then today, Sunday, we did it two more times. I don't know what is going through his head. He got a phone call from one of his girlfriends on the Internet, so I don't know what to think anymore.

Apr. 2, 2004

Well, Eric and I haven't done anything for like two weeks. He has asked and hinted it, but I can't. I like him way more than he likes me. He is hot, nice, and funny, but only when he is horny does he come walking, so I told him no. Jen and Travis are going out, and they have had sex twice, working on three, as we speak, I believe. I want someone who I truly care about and who cares about me, someone I can talk to and cuddle with, someone I can trust. I am only seventeen, about to be eighteen. I am sure I will find someone who I care about, who I love, and who loves me for me not just a quick way to get laid. Why do guys do this? Because God gave them a pole and showed them had to use it?

Apr. 5, 2004

I am really confused. I like Scott Gayton, Steve is nice, and I think I really have feelings for Eric. Eric doesn't care about me like that, and now he has a girlfriend. Scott doesn't like me either, and Steve is just a good friend. I would like a boyfriend, but being single is nice. I can do what I want, when I want. My birthday is in twenty days, and I will be eighteen, old enough to go out with whoever I want. We went camping, and Mel and Gunnar fucked again. He didn't wear a condom, and she was drunk. It wasn't right. I also have to go to the doctor's this month for my stomach, but the appointment is being sent to Tom and Janet's, so I will have to get it from her. I am tired of trying to find someone. I should give it up. It will happen when it is meant to. Mel and Gunnar no longer talk because she thinks she could be pregnant. She was so pissed off.

Apr. 9, 2004

It has been three weeks, and I am going to go insane. I come home early and stay up late. I peek under his door or move the blinds just to see if he is awake. I get up early when I hear him sneeze. I am a mess. I like him so much. I try and do anything just so he would notice me. He has hinted a few times that he wants to do something when the time comes. I feel guilty. He has a girlfriend now. I want a boyfriend. It's just I can't get one who I like. Anyways, my aunt called. She isn't sending the money she said she would. My social security stopped, and now I am broke. I wish life would give me a break. I also wish the best for Cindy and Mark, Eric, Jason, Brandon, my brothers, and everyone else who is having a hard time. May God be with you. I love you all.

Apr. 14, 2004

Life is hard. I have been paying bills and making my own decisions since I was fifteen. Most people dream of this all their life, but when it comes true, they're singing a different tune. I have been though a lot of stuff. Some people don't even know what I put up with. I have moved more times and been to more schools than I care for. My parents fought over every little thing. They hit and threw whatever was close enough that they could get their hands on, and the kids were always in the middle. They have separated and gotten back together numerous times. I have dealt with my fair share of drama and stupid stuff. I believe this changes my life for the better, though. I had to deal with my mom's death, the family fighting over us kids, going to school, and staying out of trouble. I dealt with things I have done at parties and lived with my bad choices. I have been working and paying for my bills and expenses for three years. Most kids would never go through what Jenn and I have had to do, and some have it a lot worse. God gives us all many tasks, and he sees which one falls though and how many can stick with it. I find myself depressed and thinking about my mom and how my life was before the drugs and her death, before my brother went downhill, before I got kicked out the first two times. All I know for sure is I wouldn't be here right now if it wasn't for my sister. I bust my ass in school to keep my grades so I can pay for school. I always make the wrong choices when it comes to guys. All they want is a piece of ass, or that is what I believe. That is all I ever see, so that is what I have to believe.

Apr. 15, 2004

We had sex again today. He asked if I missed him. He then asked me if I thought Katie, his new girlfriend, was cute. He asked if I would ever have a threesome with him and her. He said she had never, but she wanted to try. He then told me she thought I was cute. He said he would never stop fucking me. He said he was a big cheat because he is cheating on her with me again. April 16 and 18, we fucked again.

Mar. 26–29, 2004

This is jumping back, but Steve, Scott, Jake, Katie, Jen, Travis, Brook, and I all went to Pismo for a vacation, and it was fun. We had Brook go because we needed a twenty-one-year-old to get the rooms and to buy the alcohol. The day going down, we took three cars—Jen and Travis in the El Camino, Katie and Jake in her truck, and Scott, Steve, Brook, and I all in her car. The ride down was fun. We got out some paper. We started drawing pictures for the guys behind us. One said, "Jake, shows us you're Bobbies." Another had a picture of a donkey and a person behind it boning it in the ass. There was a stop sign coming up. Steve jumps out of the car, runs to Jake's car, puts the picture in the wiper blades, and then puts the donkey in Travis's car. Then later, there was construction being done on the road we were on. I have never seen two people so happy to be stopped because of construction. They put another picture on Jake's truck, then they put a note on Travis's car. Jake then gets out and pulls down his pants in front of a whole line of cars, including the construction workers. Well, we finally get to our hotel. It was nothing but fun the whole time. We went down to the beach, we buried Travis in the sand, and we drank every night. We played sevens, and then we played a game Scott made up. You have a deck of cards, and every number you flipped over, you took that many drinks. On the last night, we were on our own. Brook had to leave and go back to work. Jake and Katie got mad at each other and left a day early. On the day we were leaving, we drove out to the beach, then Morro Bay. We then fed the squirrels. They would eat right out of your hands. We then went to Cayucos and looked at the pier. It is all right next to Pismo. Then we headed home. All of us had a great time. Cindy and Mark let us go after a long talk and debate. They trust us on just our word. It is really nice to have two people who really care and trust you to stay in a hotel room with a couple of guys on just your word. I had a lot of fun.

April 27–28, 2004

On the twenty-fifth, we slept together again. On the twenty-seventh, Steve, Travis, Gunnar, Jen, and I all went to the lake. It was really hot. Well, we promised Gunnar $5 if he would run down the deck butt naked, screaming, "I have no legs!" Well, he did in front of a lot of people. Then we all went and grabbed his clothes and started walking to the cars. He then came running after us. He ran straight to the cars. It was really funny. This week, Jenn, Mel, Lilly, Travis, Jake, and Scott are all doing chieftains days, where you make a team of six people and you have to do like different obstacles and beat the other teams. The school has it every year toward the springtime. This normally consists of making a fool of yourself in front of the whole school. I didn't want to do it.

April 30, 2004

We had sex again, guess I will never learn

May 2, 2004

Well, today was the first day back to work. I worked from 12:00 p.m. to closing, which ended up around 8:45 p.m... Well, I finally got back to work, and our car dies the same day. That is just my luck. Oh well, hope it is something easy that won't cost more than a hundred dollars.

May 15, 2004

Today we drove to LA to watch a Dodgers' game. Eric and I fucked on the thirteenth. Although I am not a huge fan of baseball, it was still fun. Freddy Prince was there. The score was 4–0; the Dodgers lost to the Red Sox. Cindy poured beer on the back of the guy who was sitting in front of her. We got peanuts, cotton candy, and Cracker Jacks. It was a lot of fun. Jenn and I got our own hotel room. They didn't know we were all together because the last names are different, so we were on the bottom floor in the back. Cindy and Mark were in one room, and Eric and Katie were in a different one—on the second floor toward the front. I kind of want a boyfriend now. I miss the whole talking and cuddling thing, but I will find someone, soon, I hope, but when I do, it is going to be someone I like and who feels the same way. He will be mine, all mine. No more of this sleeping-around thing, meeting behind the parents' backs, and hiding it from the girlfriend. It will be really nice.

June 10, 2004

Well, graduation came and went too fast. All my relatives came up. They're staying at my workplace right now. They have two cabins, and Robert, Beth, Jojo, my aunt Ruth, and her husband, Kevin, are staying at the Pines across from the lake. My dad and Pam just came up for the day. His mom and her husband are staying at a friend's house in Fresno.

My aunt JoAnne, Phil, and Andrew are rooming with my grandma. Aunt Marry, Joey, and his girlfriend are staying in one cabin, along with Cindy. My aunt Tina, uncle Mike, Becka, and Mat are all staying in another. It wasn't too bad. After grad night, we had a barbecue at the lake, and everyone played horseshoes. My stepdad, my uncle Skeet, and Kelley showed up. My grandma on my mom's side has only said one word to me since she has been here, and that was, "Good job." She can't deal with the fact that my mom is dead and that we look like her. Like that is my fault, but whatever. She lost a daughter, and now she is losing her grandchildren over nothing. You can't mention mom's name around her, or she gets all pissed off. My dad handed Jenn and I both a check for $500 to get our car fixed, which was really nice of him. I got a lot of money from graduation, which works. Jenn and I are going to save up our money and get a place and move out, hopefully by the end of summer. We can do it now. We don't have any bills to pay, and we just got all this money. Plus both of us are working full-time. It will be really nice to move out. All the family has left or are leaving tomorrow morning. They're not getting along entirely well. They can't be under the same roof for very long, or they start bitching at one another.

July 2, 2004

Well, I haven't written in a few weeks because some very unplanned things happened. The family all left. Jen, Chris, and I went to Fresno the day after they left and had a good time. We hung out, went to lunch, and went shopping, just having some family time. The next day, Jen and I got up, got all the cans ready, and turned them in at the little place in North Fork. We were then going to Oakhurst to put our money in the account. After dropping the cans off, we decided to stop in at the Pizza Factory to eat. We left and headed to Oakhurst, but we never made it. We got into our fifth accident on the way. We were about a mile from town. We came around the corner, and our right tire blew out, causing us to go into the other lane. A car going about fifty-five hit us on the side, then we hit a tree and a pole. We had bruising on the brain, which caused us to lose our short-term memory for about nine days. I had six broken bones and was stuck in a wheelchair. Jenn had stroke-like symptoms, so she had to relearn how to walk again.

We finally got released today, but I am still in this chair. I broke my hip, pelvic, my arm, my sacrum, and two ribs. I couldn't believe it when I finally woke up. I thought I was having a dream. Not to mention, they tell me it is now nine days later. The accident was on the fifteenth. The night before the accident, we'd watched *50 First Dates*, and Eric and I had slept together.

I was so pissed off because I couldn't do anything when I got home. There are stairs at Cindy's house. There are four steps to get into the house, two from the kitchen to the living room, one to get into my room. Mark built rams, but they are too steep for me to get up them myself. I can't do anything. Then I finally get home, and Cindy goes, "You know why the guys look so sad yesterday?"

I go, "No, why?"

She goes, "Well, you know that Gunnar went up to Montana, right?"

I am all, "Yeah, he is working up there, so what is the problem?"

She said, "Well, yesterday when he was going to work, he was driving his boss's dirt bike, and his boss was coming up the dirt road and hit Gunnar on the bike. He didn't make it."

I asked, "Well, why didn't you tell me yesterday when it happened?"

She said she didn't want to disappoint us because we were coming home.

I got all pissed off. I said, "This is two different things—me coming home and one of my close friends dying at seventeen."

By this time, I am so frustrated, pissed, and sad all at the same time. I can't move around Cindy's house. There is too much stuff, and the ramps are way too steep to go anywhere. So I ask Cindy to push me into my room. She does. I ask her to just leave and shut the door and leave me alone for a little while. Jenn took off with Travis and Steve. I can't go anywhere because I am in this wheelchair, and all my friends have trucks, so I cannot get in them. I cried for a long time till I cried myself to sleep, which I have not done in a long time. Then Cindy tells me I can't go to the funeral next week because it's outside. I looked at her and told her, "I am going no matter what you say. He was my friend, who happened to like me, and I never gave him a chance."

So Jenn and my plans for this summer went out the window, like they always do. I can't work for a while, at least until I can walk again. I have never felt so empty and alone and depressed and all by myself since my mom died. I hate this feeling, that I am all alone and no one cares. July 14 is when I go in for x-rays again. Hopefully, fingers crossed, they say I can walk.

July 3, 2004

Cindy had to help me take a shower today, so I was not very happy at all. I can do it. I really don't need that much help. All I wanted to do mainly was shave my legs and wash my hair. So I cried again today. Gunnar's funeral is on the fifth. I am eighteen years old, and I am only diapers away from being two again. I can't remember anything, my talking is all messed up, and I can't stand living here. They're all pigs. We're going to watch the fireworks tomorrow. That will be fun, hopefully. Travis offers to push me in my chair. I can't get anywhere in the house without help. I can hardly dress myself, and doing my hair or makeup is a joke. The feeling of uselessness, alone and afraid, keeps me up at night and asleep all day. This was not how I was supposed to spend my last free summer.

July 14, 2004

Went to the doctor's. I still have a fracture in my pelvis, so I have to use the wheelchair or a crutch. It hurts really bad, but at least I can walk.

Nov 20, 2004

Well, Jen and Cindy had some words, and so she got pissed, and Jen left. I am caught in the middle. I don't know what to do. They both vent to me. I can't do anything. I really don't need this. I am no longer working, and I have all kinds of bills that are coming in, plus trying to find a job and go to school. I can't take this any longer. Jenn and I got into it last night. We went to Oakhurst to watch a movie. She starts on me about why I am still living there, that I can move in with her at Travis and live in the trailer with her. She asks How I am still sleeping with Eric and says it's my fault that she got kicked out. We are drifting further away. Then she goes on about me smoking, about how I am killing myself, how Eric is just using me, how it's wrong because he has a girlfriend, how nice she is and how wrong he is, and how she doesn't want to see me hurt. What she doesn't understand is how she is hurting me by yelling and telling me all this and all the ways I have been fucking up. So I am sitting here. I decided to take four of my Vicodin pills on top of my muscle relaxers. I am just trying to relax so I can go to sleep. It is now 5:00 a.m. I am smoking. I have almost finished a whole pack of smokes. I look over and see a pair of scissors sitting on my nightstand. I start cutting up paper to take my mind of my depression. I drop my cigarette on my arm and didn't feel the burn it left. I start to run the blade over my arm. It catches the burn, and it starts to bleed. For some reason, I felt better. It relieved some pain. So I go back and forth, singing along to my radio, drinking some of the alcohol I got from the kitchen. I look down at my arm, and it's now streaked with blood. I make my way to the bathroom, tripping on the dog that is deaf and blind, so it doesn't even hear me coming. I fall on my left side, and it hurt nothing like having most of your weight landing on a broken bone. Well, at this time, I have a buzz, and I have two cigarettes left. So I grab the rubbing alcohol out of the cabinet and pour it on my arm. It burns pretty badly. I turn around to go back to my room. I start getting dizzy. It could be from the different kinds of alcohol I just drank or the pills I took forty-five minutes ago. I turn back around and head for the front door, where I find myself sitting on the front steps, throwing up. I start to cry, thinking about all the people I have once cared about who are now gone. Then I start hearing the same voices. It sounds like my sister and a man talking, so I get up and start to walk around the house. It's windy outside, so I blame it on that. I go back to my room, finish drinking, and then I hear them again. I brush it off and try to get some sleep

Everyone is asking where I got the scar on my wrist from. I make up some lie and say I got it on the stove at

Cindy's one morning when I was cleaning. I told them I didn't know it was hot. Today I am going to Fresno to give my brother some papers. I stopped at a Chevron because I really had to pee. Jenn points out a paper on the door that says they are hiring, so I asked the lady at the register for an application. She seems nice and hands me one. Daniel is working with her. He knows my brother.

Dec. 23, 2004

I have to go back to Fresno today to pay a bill because one of my checks bounced and they need the cash. I figure since I need to drive back by the Chevron, I can take my application in and dropped it off. I go in, and Megan, who I went to school with, is standing at the register. I hand her my application, and she asks if I want to talk to the owner because he was there. I take a look at what I was wearing, and I am in my pajama pants and a shirt. She says, "They won't care," so I said, "Sure." I go to the back, where the guys are. I sit at the table, and then later, I find out it was her dad. So I have to have an interview in my pj's. When I was done, I walked back out to the car. Travis goes, "So how was your interview?" I asked how he knew, and he laughed.

Dec. 29, 2004

Bruce called and wants me to come in on the thirty-first to start work. I was excited.

Jan. 10, 2005

Work is going well. I cook and work at the store once a week, so I am on the schedule twice a week, getting to know the regulars who are always here. There is a guy named Chester. He seems really nice. Then there is another guy named Scott.

I am working the night shift with the lady who I got the application from. Her name is Debbie, and Scott is in. He only lives next door and takes a break from the house and comes to the chevron to hang out He seems really nice. Debbie is showing me how to close and what I need to do. I am wiping down the cupboards, and the two of them are cracking jokes. I pretend not to catch on, like I don't know what they are talking about. Well, Scott sees me laughing and says, "Look at her just giggling over there."

I look up and say, "I don't know what you are talking about." We close, and I go home. Eric is up, and he texts to see if "I want to play." That's what he calls it. I tell him I don't know, and the day at work is all I can think about. Scott gets my phone number and keeps calling it, driving me crazy because I don't know who it is, so I finally just call back. He acts like it was just a joke, but we end up talking for a few hours, and then I tell him I have to go because I had to work early.

Chapter 5

Jan. 20, 2005

Scott's birthday is coming up, and he asked if I wanted to stop by after work with Debbie and have some drinks. Michal Paul, his girlfriend, Daniel, and Monica are all going to be there as well. Usually I would have said no, but something about him made me agree.

Jan. 26, 2005

Well, today I got ready for work. I drove down after telling Cindy I would either be home late or not at all. I showed up at work, and they had changed the schedule and didn't call and tell me. They took me off the night shift and moved me to Thursday morning, which is tomorrow, so I go home, change, and took Jenn, Travis, and Tyson to go with me. Well, the other night, we all went out drinking, and I was bored, so I called Scott on my cell phone when we were at Central Camp. We were talking for a while, and then my phone died, so when I got home, I called him back, but I only had his cell number. Everyone cut out early, so I took the rest of the beer into my room and drank it, talking to him. It was like three in the morning when we finally hung up. Well as I was talking to him, Eric was texting me on the cell phone. I was playing stupid and acted like I had no clue on what he wanted. Well, we hung up on the phone, and I was asleep, so I didn't answer. I wake up about thirty minutes later, and Eric is in my room. I asked what he was doing, and he said, "Nothing, now I got what I wanted," whatever that is supposed to mean. I don't think I really passed out. I was just tired.

Well, anyways, back to the birthday. Jenn, Travis, Tyson, and I are at Scott's really early. He is making a few drinks, and I am kind of flirting with him like I always do. Well, Daniel and Monica show up, and Travis, Jen, and Tyson leave. Daniel and Scott go to make a drink, and Monica asks if there is anything going on between the two of us. I told her no, that we are just friends. Well, the night goes on, and I am drinking more. I got to thinking, "What if?" Well Debbie and MP get off work, and they show up, and Scott and I are sitting next to each other. I keep accidentally burning him with my cigarette. Well, it hits 3:00 a.m., and I stop drinking because I have to be at work at six. Everyone left at four, and I was staying the night. I went and lay on the couch, and then Scott came in and sat down next to me, so I moved and put my head in his lap. I was not going to go to sleep because I figured I would be more tired when I woke up. Then Scott moves over to the other side of the couch and lies down, so I moved and lay next to him. I had a blue tank top on that was nice and soft. Well, Scott had his hand on my stomach. Then he started rubbing it, and I wanted to see if he would do anything because most guys would be all over that the moment you lay down. But he didn't. It felt so nice to be able to lie down next to a guy who wasn't trying to get into your pants every opportunity they got. I felt so relieved and comfortable. Time to get up and go to work.

Jan. 27, 2005

All day at work, I was thinking about how I was flirting and me lying next to him. He told me I could go back over and take a nap so I would not drive home tired. After work, I went home, mostly because I was nervous from the night before. I get home, and Eric is the only one there. I am tired. Well, he follows me into my room and starts taking off his clothes as I am lying in my bed with no pants on. Well, we have sex, and the whole time, I can only think of last night and how Scott didn't try and do anything. He just lay there, and he was a true gentleman. Almost every time there are guys around and they're drinking, I almost have to fight off at least one. I am not trying to brag, but most of the time, it is because guys have a one-track mind; they see boobs, and they try and get it. Well, as soon as Eric finished, he left. That made me wonder why I do it. Why do I put up with it? It is a complete waste of time.

Feb. 2, 2005

Well, Scott and I have been talking a long time on the phone. We text almost every night, and I go over after work a few times. Well, he said he is going to have a few more people over and asked if I wanted to go, so I told him I did. Well, this time, I didn't have to work in the morning, but I stayed the night again. I was lying in his room on his bed, and he starts to rub my back. I have never had a guy rub my back without me having to ask or anything. It was great, especially since I fractured my lower back in the car accident. I found out a bit of information on him. He was once married. He has twin girls who are fourteen, and he works at home making gold crowns for teeth. He reminds me of myself, which could be a good thing. I am not quite sure. I don't know if he likes me more than a friend or not, but I think I might actually like him. We have not had sex, and that is perfectly okay. I stopped seeing Eric because it is a complete waste of my time. He can fuck something else for a long time.

Feb. 3 through March 20, 2005

Well, Scott and I have had sex a few times. The second time we did, I was laughing at him when we were finished. I am no longer on the pill, so he should have worn a condom. Well, the first time, he was going to put one on but never got around to it. The second time, there was one under the pillow,

I had one under the phone, and I had some in my purse next to the bed, and he didn't use one. Well, I got up went to the bathroom and came back. He was sitting on the edge of the bed smoking a cigarette. I asked him what was wrong. He stands up, reaches under the bed, grabs his gun, takes it out of the case, and says, "I am so retarded. I am surrounded by condoms. I might as well give the gun to Robert [who is my older brother; Scott, at this time, does not know the story from when I was younger] and have him pull the trigger, or I could pay the kids." I was laughing. I thought it was funny. I had already gotten my birth control, but I couldn't start taking it yet. I had to start my period again and then wait until Sunday came along. Then Scott goes, "Yeah, if you have it." Well, I wasn't really worried about it.

June 9, 2005

Well, today Travis had graduation because he is a year behind Jen and me. I have the whole day off, so I go up to North Fork, Jen and I went to Oakhurst. Well, we refilled our prescriptions, and I bought a pregnancy test. We went to the graduation, and then Travis, Jen, JJ, and Katie all followed me back to Scott's, where I am now living. I had Jen take the test before we started drinking. It came back positive. She was so mad. Well, they all ended up staying the night, and she got up and took another one to see if it was right. So my sister is pregnant. They are going to wait before they tell Misty (Travis's mom), and Jen asked me not to tell anyone.

So I moved in with Scott. I went ahead and told Cindy she can have the room that I am staying in because I am never home and that I was staying with Debbie from work because she would probably disapprove of me and Scott, I think, not really sure. I went ahead and moved out, but I left on good terms, and I stop by every once in a while. Eric finally got it through his head that it is over. He asked if we were ever going to "play again," and I told him no. Then I left. Well, Scott and I went to Santa Cruz, and we had a lot of fun. We rode on the rides, walked through the sand, and walked on the pier. I really love him, and I hope it lasts. I get along with his kids, and his dad works on my teeth, and he didn't charge me anything for it. I have not met his mom, but his dad seems really nice. I trust Scott more than I have ever trusted any guy before in my life. He might be forty-eight years old, but he doesn't act like it. More than half the time, I think we are the same age in spirit.

June 19, 2005

Well, today is Father's Day. Scott, Erika, Nicole, and I went to Hometown Buffet, then we went to his dad's house to wish him a happy Father's Day. I was kind of shy when we got there because I have only meet his dad twice—once when he looked at my wisdom teeth and gave me a referral and then once when he had my teeth cleaned. So I went over, and on the fourteenth. I had my last three wisdom teeth pulled, so my mouth was kind of sore. I called my real dad today to wish him a happy Father's Day, and Jen told me to tell him she was pregnant, so I did. He didn't seem mad or anything. Jen only wanted one person to be happy for her, and he just degraded her boyfriend with Robert. Travis told Robert yesterday by accident. he thought he was texting back and forth with Beth. I told my aunt JoAnne for her, and she was so happy, to my surprise.

July 1, 2005

It has been one year since Gunnar was killed and one year since are accident, and I have to work. Jenn, Travis, Katie, and Justin are going to go camping where we always went with Gunnar. I miss him a lot. He was a good friend, even if Cindy didn't like him or want him at her house. He changed from the last time he had an encounter with her, but she could not see that. Whenever I start to miss him, I just think of all the fun times we all had together.

July 8, 2005

Well, I have to go to work in about an hour, and Scott went to pick up the kids from summer school. Tomorrow is my mom's four-year death anniversary. Jenn, Travis, Scott, and I are going somewhere to eat. Have not found out where yet. I have to work from 5:30 a.m. to 3:00 p.m., and Jen has to work until eight tomorrow, so we're going to a late dinner. I miss her every day. I pray she is happy and that I don't disappoint her. Jen is saving up money for her new baby. She has $700 saved, and she has been putting $100 away every paycheck since May. Travis is putting money away for a place, so I think they can pull it off. Robert and my dad don't think they can do it. He calls Travis a loser and everything. Not too many people are happy for her, and it's sad. She is trying her best. It is what it is. We ended up going to Red Lobster. Had a lot of fun.

Aug. 6, 2005

Well, today is Saturday. I got up for work at four. My aunt JoAnne, Phil, and Andrew are coming up. They are staying at Jenn's. Well, after work, they came down for a barbecue. Well, I was not smoking in front of them, so I would get up and leave to smoke a cigarette. Well, that meant leaving Scott out there with JoAnne and Phil. I then headed back outside to where they were. Nicole called me over to look at Travis's nails, and then we started talking about JoAnne and everything. Then I remembered Scott was still out there, and so I told Jenn to tell him to get dessert so he can get away. So she does. We all eat the dessert, and they leave. Well, I was talking to Nicole and Eka about what they thought, then I said I was sorry for leaving Scott out there by himself, and I said, "I had to." Well, that must have set him off, and now he is not talking to me. I didn't do it on purpose. I don't think it is going to last between him and me. I love him so much. I tell everyone about him. I am happy when I am around him. That right there should be enough to stay, but I don't think I can deal with all the stuff, like having to be right next to him the whole time, being right by his side. It's not that I don't want to be, but my aunt got me thinking about what she said, about how he is so much older. I want to be able to have my fun without him wondering if I am seeing someone else or what I am going to do with my life. Do I really want to be thirty-eight and taking care of someone who is sixty-eight? I don't care right now. I am so much happier now that I have met him. I live with him, and I love his kids, although I won't be able to have my own. I treat them with all the respect in the world, the same with Scott. I love him so much. I hope all this changes. It would be a whole lot easier. Good night.

Aug. 16, 2005

Well, thinking it over for about two seconds, I have come to the realization that I can do without having a kid. I don't want to go through the pregnancy, for sure. If I get desperate, I will watch Jen's kid. That would change my mind in a heartbeat. Don't get me wrong, kids are okay. If you can get them at eighteen, and they leave when they want.

Oct. 27, 2005

Well, Halloween is about here, and we are going to have a haunted house. I think it's going to be really cool. Well, Suzie is taking some time off work because she might be leaving her husband. I don't think she is coming back; she is going to be staying with her mom. If I was her, I wouldn't come back. All her kids are raised, and she is not happy. I love where I am at in my life. I am happy, and everything is going good.

Chapter 6

Feb. 6, 2006

Well, I have not written in a long time. Starting where I left off, we had the haunted house, and it went fine. There were a lot of kids over to help out, and Scott invited a friend over as well. Her name is Joy, and she is a really nice lady. Then in December, I spent way too much money on the kids and my sister's family. It was worth every penny. On December 4, Scott bought two tickets to see Reba, the country singer, live on stage at Table Mountain Casino. It was a lot of fun. They played a lot of songs, and she sang "Sister," one of my favorite songs. We bought a huge Christmas tree, which we had to put on Scott's car. I spent $101.77 on it, and it was about eleven and a half feet tall. We put it in the living room and decorated it with tons of ornaments.

I can't remember if I had mentioned it yet, but his parents and I are getting along great. Kent even called and apologized right before Halloween for the way he had been acting, and Scott, his mom, and I all went out to eat breakfast. That was when I first met her.

Christmas went well. Scott and I lay in bed until about 11:00 a.m. Then we got up opened the gifts that we got and waited for his kids to come over. Jen and Travis came over that night. Two weeks before Christmas, Suzie got fired from the Chevron. She came back, had some words with Trina, and put a dead jackrabbit on Brender's silver Mustang. He is a vegetarian, and he does not like meat. Mike hired Robin back.

January came and went, and then it was February. On the second of this month is Scott's and my one-year anniversary. I tried and played it off like I forgot like I have a couple times in the past. On the thirty-first of January, I went up to Cindy's for dinner. On the way home, I went up to Oakhurst and picked up a two-hundred-piece tool kit because most of his tools are broken or got stolen, and he doesn't really need a whole lot.

Well, that night when I got off work, he gave me my present. I opened up the small square box. Inside was a ring, and what this ring means is that it's a thought in the right direction. It's a preengagement ring or a promise ring, whichever one you are familiar with. It can't be anything more because of his parents, kids, and ex-wife. It's too early for the parents, the kids have enough stress in school, it wouldn't be fair to add one more thing, and then his child support checks would stop. So I am perfectly happy with a promise ring. I don't mind waiting.

Jen is almost about to explode. She almost had the baby on the third. She was 1 cm dilated, so they waited, and she is coming up tomorrow to go walking with me. So we will say bye for now and good night.

Mar. 27, 2006

Tomorrow Scott and I were planning on going to Oregon to buy a boat. I was putting $1,600 in, and Kent was putting the rest in. Well, this morning we found out Kent doesn't have the money to do it, and we can't do it alone, so there will be no boat. Scott has been working like crazy trying to get all his work done so we could go. Well, he is all mad or bummed out. He really wanted this. He has not had a good four hours of sleep since Friday. It is now Monday night. I am in the room right now because he is on edge. My plan is save up as much as possible so he can get a boat like the one he saw. He really likes it. By June, I would have about $1,700. By next summer, I should have a nice down payment for his dream boat.

Chapter 7

May 2, 2009

Okay, so it's been three years since I have written in this. A lot has happened. Today Scott and I are getting married. We are having a small wedding in the backyard, mostly family. My sister came from Colorado, and my real dad came. My stepdad made it too. My brother Chris and his girlfriend came, and a few friends, Scott's family. It turned out really nice. There was a small chance of rain, but it only sprinkled and then went away. Scott's mom helped out a lot.

I lost a lot of weight for my dress. Got down to 132. Had paid for three months of training beforehand. I looked hot. The only thing I wish I would have done was had a few more people, some work friends, but we were trying to keep it small. Scott didn't want to spend too much, and he was doing all the cooking. He didn't want to deal with my workpeople, claimed it would cause to much drama and unwanted quests.

Told Scott about six months ago that last year I cheated on him and I was calling it off, but he begged me to stay and said that we would work it out, and so I gave it a lot of thought. We talked. He said he can get through it and promised me after we got married, I could have a kid, so I get to try and have a family now. By the way, we did get a boat. We took it out a couple of times and absolutely love it. I paid $1,600 for it. Not bad for a bass fishing boat. Everything was going well; he was actually giving me freedom, and we were not fighting. He said once I finished school, we could work on having a baby, and I hope we do.

Nov. 8, 2009

Today Elizabeth was born, Jen's second baby. Her and Travis had a baby boy four years earlier in February. She was about four months pregnant at my wedding. Me? Still no kids. Scott keeps pushing it back. Says when I am done with school or when I make more money or this or that, Well, I am almost done with my schooling, and now it's time to decide what to do with the rest of my life. I now work at Vons. Been here for a few years, and I love it, but I would be better off not being here.

Dec. 25, 2009

Today is Christmas day, and I just got off of work, which I volunteered to do because of the extra money. Not to mention we don't do anything. Still no kids and no sign or thought of one. Getting bitter, and we seem to fight more and more about little things. Not sure why. Think he still holds anger about me cheating the few years earlier. He really doesn't trust me to do anything or go anywhere anymore. He did make a nice dinner tonight. Have to get up early and go back to work. Not sure how I got that short end of the stick.

Chapter 8

May 22, 2010

Today my brother and his girlfriend Cheyenne got married; it was a very nice wedding. They are expecting their first child. It's so exciting. Brother is so happy. My real dad showed up, and my stepdad, sister, and her family were all there. It was so nice had it at Shaver Lake in a small church. Tomorrow I go to the doctor's for my CT. Already had an MRI, and all results are clear. Story of my life. I just can't get rid of the headaches. Scott's and my anniversary came and went. We did not do anything special. My dad wanted to come over for dinner, so we had dinner here at the house. Scott's mom gave us a check for $2,500, which helped a lot. Scott has not been doing to well on his work, and business slowed down a lot, so my whole check goes to paying the household bills, which is a new one, because normally my checks went for emergency funds or to pay stuff off.

Nov. 1, 2010

Well, today, I just had enough. I can't do this anymore. I have tried and tried to get past it, tried to convince myself that I don't want kids, that they just cost money, that they get in the way, and that this would be better for my marriage, but I am done. So today I told Scott I was done. I wanted out and said that I didn't want to live like this. The truth is, he does not trust me, and he holds me back like a prisoner, makes me feel worthless, like I can't do anything, like I am not going to go anywhere. I have built up so much regret and tension toward him after three years of him telling me we can have kids when this happens or when that happens. Well, I am done. I am done waiting and busting my ass trying to achieve a goal that is so far out of reach in his lifetime. Then the second I say I am done, he brings up the having a kid.

"Well, I thought we were going to have kids?"

Is he serious? I have been waiting for three years and nothing! We fight over this month after month, and then once I have accepted the reality of never having kids and have mentally prepared myself of only being the aunt and never the mom, he mentions the kids? Really!

So then I tell him I am moving out. Now I'm only staying here till I have the money to move out. I think he is making that impossible. He keeps bringing up extra expenses. Like he is just making it that much more difficult for me to have any extra money to move.

Nov. 7, 2010

So today on the way to work, I decided to drive to a friend's house. Well, not knowing anything, I went to work. After work, I went and had coffee with an old friend. Later, I come to find out Scott followed me to work and then to my friend's house. Mind you, this is two o'clock in the morning. I just needed someone to look at me with the eyes that say that no one else in the world matters, that I was the most beautiful thing he had ever seen. I can talk to my friend about anything. He just sits there and listens. Doesn't say anything, just listens like Scott used to do when we first met. He does the things that I want to do. I want to go out, I don't want to have to call and ask for permission to go to lunch with the girls, and I don't want to feel like I am on house arrest. The only thing that is missing is the ' monitor. I can't take it anymore. Yeah, I felt bad that he had to drive by and see my car there in the driveway of another man. Although in all fairness, I told him we were done. He asked me to stay until he had time to processes it all, but he still floored me. At 2:00 a.m., the last thing I would be doing is following someone to work thirty miles away from our house, then going an extra ten minutes from there. That's way too much time. The man is controlling and needs someone who likes that and does not want to go anywhere or do anything. My sis would be perfect for him. She is too embarrassed to leave the house. I hate my life and myself.

Nov. 15, 2010

So as the days go on, I feel like killing myself every day. I think of different ways I could do it. I don't know if it's because of all the medicine I am on or simply because I just can't take it anymore, this pain I feel every day in my body, in my heart. I can't have what I want. I thought by now I would have a child, that I would be happy, but now I am just trying to save enough money to move out and start something, whatever that is. I just want peace and quiet, to wake up and have some time to myself. I would crawl out of bed and not have someone following every step I take. I could relax and just have five minutes and lie on the couch if I want to. That's what I want. I love my husband, but I just need time to breathe, to think, to not be bothered so I can find myself, to be on my own, to live or to end it without having someone watching my every second of the day. I want Scott not to show up on breaks or lunches, after work, or just stop by unannounced to see if I am at work. He acts like I am his daughter instead of his wife. His kids have more freedom than I have. He promises me a baby, and he waits until the moment I say I want out to tell me that he's ready? What kind of mind game is that? I can't take it. I think I am going to wait to see if I am pregnant, and if I am not this month, then I am going to try one more time, but it will be on a day off, so I will write in a couple days before anything happens because with my luck,

I am pretty sure I am cursed. God hates me, and he wants me to be miserable for something that I guess I did in this lifetime or in a different one. Good night.

Nov. 22, 2010

So I started a couple of days ago. I think about the other person, like, every day, and I don't know why. I just want something different, I guess, and I am holding on to nothing. Scott won't let me leave this place, no matter how many times I tell him, no matter how many fights we have, maybe even if he finds out that I have cheated. I have just given up. So after the holidays, I want out of this world. I don't make enough or have the qualifications to rent something without a cosigner, and Scott won't sign. I don't understand. I told him I will still be around. I just need to figure things out on my own. I need to live a little, be a twenty-four-year-old. I think I moved in and married him because he gave me the protection and the comfort of a father, which I didn't have. Now I want to remain friends because I don't want to lose his family. His mom has become a mom to me. I wish this was easy, so I could just take myself out of this place, and no one would get hurt. No one is really to blame but me.

I do miss this other person, though. He won't tell me how he feels because I go home to Scott. I don't blame him. I just feel bad that I got him in the middle of my fucked-up and disorganized life. He wants me to be happy, and he thinks that moving out would give me that while Scott thinks I should stay here, but he is driving me nuts, and being in this house, I can't be happy. I put on a smile, but it's really just hiding all the pain in my heart. I wish I had a gun. I would just pull the trigger and get it over with. I don't care anymore, but I think pills are easier and quieter. I don't know where I went so wrong. I was happy being with Scott five years ago, but I was young, and he trusted me, and then the problems started when I went to work at Vons. I cheated, and then I told him, and then it just kept getting worse. There is no end in sight. I hate my life and every decision that has gotten me to this point, the point that I am in right now. I miss my mom, I miss the sex that used to take place on that cold morning with the other person before work—I miss it all. Scott doesn't give me a chance to miss anything. He is always here, always wanting to know what I am doing, where I am going (inside the house), what I am writing, etc. It's too much. I am drowning.

Dec. 2, 2010

So tonight is the night. So far, I have been called a "low-life scum, a cheating whore, a bitch, slut", and the list goes on. I might be out this weekend, hopefully. I have the weekend off. It would be the perfect time. Maybe this time it will work out if I planned on ending it. I just have to make sure

I don't throw up the pills this time. Last time, I think it would have worked, but I had to work, and so when I woke up, I got sick.

I might lose my job, thanks to Scott. He thinks causing my friend to lose his job would make him feel better, but that comes down to me and Margrie and him, so that is not just one person. That is three people in all to get even with. We will see how this weekend goes. Scott thinks I am completely fucked up and that I need counseling, and he says that he is done with me until I can fix myself. Thinks I can't love anyone until I love myself, and he thinks I should stay out of all relationships until I fix whatever is wrong with me. Now I am in trouble again because I told my coworkers and Jen about Scott knowing that I cheated, and so Scott got mad because I told them, said it was none of their business, and now he looks like the fool for sticking around with me. I can never win. Not sure why I waited this long. Scott keeps saying, "I know you have issues because you were raped and were molested and your mom died and your dad kicked you out and Tom and Janet kicked you out. For him, that means I have abandonment issues and so on. I don't understand why I can't do anything right and why I messed up everything I had going good for me. I guess I just was not meant to be happy. I was meant to live a long and very miserable life. Or like Scott said, "I hope you get pregnant and have a miscarriage." Not a very nice thing to say to someone who really wants kids.

Dec. 3, 2010

So after last night's conversation, Scott thinks I cheated on him with, like, four different people, which he was pissed about, but that makes it easier. He won't try and forgive me for this one. If he thinks I have been with four people while with him, then he will hate me enough, and I could never break his heart again. In reality, I have only cheated with one other man, but still, that is too much. I can't be the woman he needs, so it's best for me to let him move on and find someone who can love him like he needs and deserves, someone who has already had kids, someone who has their life together. So we will finish our talk today, and then I guess I will decide what I am going to do this weekend. I know that Saturday night and Sunday, we will probably go to the casino. Supposed to meet Jenn and Travis there Saturday, and Scott wants to go Sunday.

Dec. 12, 2010

So as you probably guessed, I am still here. He wrote this letter saying he forgives me for everything, and I was going to move in with John, and he was okay with that, but then after a couple of days, I decided to move in with sister. Then the day before the move, I mentioned it, and he flips out, saying all this stuff, like I always make bad decisions and it would be better if I went to John's instead. Then I asked what the difference is. I thought he would like it better if I moved in with sister instead of John. Then he said if I leave, we won't stay friends, and I would never be allowed back, and he will never forgive me. I don't understand. I am so completely stressed out. My hair is falling out. I can't sleep well anymore, I don't smile anymore, and I hate everything. I constantly think about what if and if it could work and maybe. Then I get text messages saying, "Please just give me a shot, see if we would work out. I will give you what you want" and "I think I can make you smile again." I don't know what to do. I think killing myself would make it much easier on everyone. Then all the hurt and confusion would be gone. The pain would go away. Both people would move on one day. I won't be happy here. That is a fact, but with the mind games, I can't leave. I am trapped in my own marriage. He is the one who claims I should not be in any relationship, yet he won't let me go. I hate my life, my job, and everything I do. I am tired all the time. I hate going to work now, but I hate being home. My friends don't want to hang out with me, and my sister's always got something she is doing, or she is too far away. I want my life back, my freedom, and my space. I want to be me again. I just want to be free. I miss him every day.

Dec. 20, 2010

Yesterday I went and saw him. I had to. He should know that I am stupid and that I can't decide anything, that I am scared of making a decision or whatever the case may be. After this month, though, I am through. I am going to try and end my life. Although I got a new car, Scott can just sell it, I suppose, and do whatever he wishes with it. Scott and I hardly have sex anymore, and when we do, I just wish for it to be over as soon as possible. I'd rather not get any at all. I would rather be with John and friends with Scott, but he will not have it that way, so I am just stuck. I can't have what I want. To be honest, I would just rather be with John, and I don't care about being friends, but I have been married, and I love him and his family. I don't want to lose it all. Oh well, that's life, I guess.

Dec. 21, 2010

So Scott's dad has been in the hospital for seven days now with heart failure, and he has a hard time trying to remember things and breathing. It doesn't look good. John is getting impatient with me because he wants me to move in, and I don't know what I am doing. I am afraid. So who knows? He is mad, and I am irritated with him. Scott's at the hospital with his dad, so I am pretty sure after Christmas on my next day off, I will just make the decision easier on everyone. I now have John texting me and saying, "Don't be mad, pretty girl. I was just asking. I won't bug you anymore about it." It's the third one he has sent. I don't know what to do. How come the decisions that I think are the best always have to be the hardest, and how come I can never be happy? Why does nothing ever go the way I want it to? My dream life would be to be with John and to have a couple kids running around. I would love to have Scott's personality and John's ability in bed. That would be one awesome mix of a man, but that will never happen. Then it is not all about the sex either. It's just I think the bridge between Scott and me is already burned, and there is nothing left—no passion, no romance, nothing. I have cheated on him. I have broken his heart, his trust, everything there is to a relationship that holds it together, I have broken it, ruined it, torn it apart.

Chapter 9

Jan. 3, 2011

So today I sit here and wonder what is wrong with me. I had my doctor's appointment and told him I wanted off on all the medicine I am on. To my surprise, he completely agreed with me and without hesitation told me what to do. As far as my love life or lack thereof, New Year's eve, I went out with a couple of people from work, got to drinking, and drank too much. I didn't want to drive at that point in time, so I went back to John's. We had the most amazing sex ever. I must have fallen asleep for about thirty minutes and woke up to my phone going off. It was Scott. He had sent me a text asking what I was doing and where I was. Then I looked at John, and he had scratches on his back and his chest. It was funny. Got him to take me back to my car. By the time I got home, it was late, and I knew I was going to be in trouble, as I should be, but to my surprise, Scott thought we were going to stay together and that everything was fine. Well, I could stay here and make him happy, but that's not really what I want. For once in a really long time, I want to do what is going to make me happy. Even if I sit back and evaluate the options, yes, Scott is the best option, and it should not matter what I want, but it's my life. I want to be happy. I want to at least see where the road takes me. Even if John and I don't work out, at least I tried, and I can move on from there. I love my husband. I just don't want to be with him anymore. Maybe I am afraid of commitment. Maybe I married him because I felt sorry, I don't know. I do know the easy way out would be to take a bunch of pills, load a gun, and pull the trigger. I probably couldn't even do that right, and I would end up in a hospital for the rest of my life. Who knows? All I know is its time to get up and make my own decisions for my happiness and see who is standing at the end of the line.

Jan. 26, 2011

Well, before this entry, I let John read this (the paper version), and he wrote on the next page, "I love you" with a smiley face. So on January 8, Jen, Travis, Scott, and I went to the casino. John texted me, so I responded to his message in front of Scott. Well, Scott gets pissed and tells me to tell John to fuck off. He says to tell the lowlife that he needed to stop texting, that I was out with my husband, and that he needed to have some 'respect. Well the truth is, I don't want to tell John to stop texting. I have feelings for him, and I think Scott is an angry man who hates everything he can't control. So needless to say, my sister and Travis left. Scott still had money left, so I asked him what he was going to play. He wants to start fighting about me and John in the middle of the casino, and I told him, "No, either play or let's leave."

He kept at it, so I told him, "Just play or get your jacket."

He said, "Who you think you are talking to me like that? You're just a fuckin' slut with no respect!"

So I started walking toward the door. He followed and said, "What do you think you're doing? I am not ready to leave."

I said, "That's fine, but I am out," and headed for the door.

He said, "What? You just going to walk off in the middle of the night?"

I said someone will give me a ride to wherever I want to go.

So he said, "Wait, let me get my jacket."

I told him, "Then go get it. I will be at the car."

I wouldn't argue in the car because my parents always did that, but he wanted to fight, calling me names, saying a bunch of stuff about John. He wants to know why I like him and tells me I can find someone better and on and on. So we get home, and I go to the bedroom and start grabbing clothes. I am done. I want out. I am over the fighting and always bringing up John and asking questions on why. I can't explain why. If I could, I would have made a decision by now. So I get in the car, and now he won't let me leave.

He grabs the garage door opener and closes the door. He says, "You are not going anywhere. Come back inside so we can talk."

What else is there to talk about? What does he want to hear? That I love John and that's where I was going? I don't know what he wants.

So he is in my car, as I try to put it in reverse. I told Scott, "I will run into the door, I don't care."

Well, he takes the door and slams it into the wall, and there goes the paint. I told him he had five minutes to move and open the garage door, or I was calling the police. He finally moved, and as I drove out of the garage, I started crying. I got to the corner to get gas, and he calls my phone. I don't answer, then he texts. He says he is sorry and that he didn't want it to end like this and that we can talk when I go back Monday to get the rest of my stuff. I arrive at John's, and he is at home, so I wipe my face and go inside. He is drunk, and we have sex and go to bed.

Then on the ninth of January, I had to go to work. John and I woke up, and we had sex again, and he went and got breakfast. I was eating and, for some reason, had to fight back tears. While I was at work again, I had to fight back tears, then I remembered Scott wanted to go to the casino that night for the birthday drawing, so I texted him and asked if he still wanted to go, and he said yes. I felt bad that I lied to John. I told him I was going to watch my sister's kids and that since it was late when we got back to the house, I just stayed the night because John had to work early and I didn't want to wake him up.

Then I went home (back to John's) after I cleaned Lloyd's house, and we had sex again. Since I was on vacation, I had the whole week off. Tuesday, John got up for work, so I cleaned the bathroom. I got scared that maybe I made a mistake and packed up my bags. I was bored, and I should have moved when I was working so I didn't have a lot of time to sit and think. While I was packing, I thought about killing myself again, so I looked around John's house to see what he had. There must be something wrong with me. I finally got out, and I still think about ending my life…So I grab my stuff, and I headed back to Scott's house. I then went and saw John on Thursday. We talked a little, had sex, and I went back to Scott's, where, to my surprise, we have sex too.

Scott asked if I had sex with John when I went over there, and I said no. He says, "Good, now move back in with me. You can save money and then decide what you want to do."

Well, I feel bad because John thinks I am with my sister, and so he still texts me and wants me to come back. I love and miss him, and after I moved back in with Scott, I realize that I still miss John. The thing is, I dream about John every time I sleep. I constantly check my phone to see if he has written. I will be going back to work soon.

John keeps texting me. Scott is getting mad. He said, "You won't tell your boyfriend you're back with your husband?" So we argue on Friday, the twenty-first, about this, and he said I was playing both sides, that I was afraid of calling it off with John because I needed people to love me and that I needed to love myself before I could even try to love anyone else, which is not true. So on the twenty-second, I wrote John and told him he needed to move on and find someone who can give him what he wants and deserves, and he said we needed to talk in person. I really felt bad. I don't want to lose John, and I want to try and make it work. I am just scared.

So on Saturday, the twenty-third, I went to John's after work so we could talk. I told him that I moved back in with Scott, and he told me to take my time on making a decision and that he would wait no matter how long and that he wants to be with me. We ended up having sex, and Scott said I could stay in his house. We wouldn't have sex, but I couldn't have sex with anyone either. See the thing is, I am not on the pill anymore, have not been for about five months, because my neurologist thinks that it's causing my headaches to be more intense and the meds that he put me on not to work. Although John does not know this, and he would probably hate me if he did find out, Scott said he was going to tell him and the fact that I am trying to trick him into getting me pregnant and that I slept with like four or five other people, but the truth is, I have only been with two people in the last seven years, and John knows that I lied to Scott about that.

So back to today, the twenty-sixth. It's Scott's birthday, and last night when I got off work, I had to swing by John's and pick up my book. I let him read this book because he wanted to see how I think and what I think about everything that has happened. He did not like the parts about me trying to kill myself, and even though I told him he couldn't judge or say anything, he still said I needed to quit talking about that because if anything happened, it would make him feel guilt. Not sure why. Then Scott and I went to the casino, and I parked my ass at the bar. Scott keeps saying stuff like I was getting fat and that I put on weight and that if I just loved him, everything would be okay. Then today he said, "If we plan on staying together, you should get life insurance out on me."

What...I don't want him. How are things supposed to be okay after everything that was said and the yelling? How do you go back? You don't! I hate when we have sex. It really makes me feel like I am being raped all over again, or should I say violated. Seriously after we have sex, I feel horrible, and it's not the age difference or the fact that John's older, and I I don't feel anything of the sort when we are done. I really miss John. I don't miss the snoring, though, but I can work past that.

My sister and her kids came over today, and it was nice. We had steak, chicken, and corn while watching Nick on the game and Elizabeth running around. It was nice. We talked about what we would be doing if she didn't have

Nick and if she and Travis didn't get married. We were supposed to move in together and go to school. Oh, how lives could have been much different than they are now.

Feb. 11, 2011

Talk about a blast from the past! So yesterday, I was at the emergency room where my nephew was a patient. He was at Yosemite High School in Oakhurst with his dad and cousins and decided he was going to run up these bleachers. He got to the top one, and it happened to be a little wet and slippery, sending him right off the back. He fell about six feet on his face, hitting the fence and the concrete below. He broke his arm, fractured his head, and gave himself a black eye and a lot of scratches.

Well, Eric has texted me saying how he missed me, and he wanted to know what I was doing. Told him, "Just been working." He then said he has been thinking about me lately and then managed to irritate me by writing, "So you want to ride on my dick?" Now come on, who writes that? I have not talked to him in over a year, and it's been probably two years since I've last seen him. So instead of answering the question, I asked if he was still with Tiffany. He said yes, and if I didn't want to do anything, then he will understand. It's just that he missed me.

Now really, I fell for this guy even though we were supposed to be just friends with benefits, and when I had seen him at his parents' going-away party, he tells me how he liked me and felt bad that he was just having sex with me and that he never told me how he really felt and that he wished I would have stayed. I just thought to myself, *You wait until after I get married to tell me this?* If he only knew how I really felt. The reason I ran when I did was because I was falling too much for him, and I figured it would not work. Then you have John, who desperately wants me to move in. He still won't tell me how he truly feels about me, and so I gave up asking.

Then my husband and I are getting along for now. We are not sleeping together, but we are not fighting either. One of the girls at work made a comment, "What do you do to these guys? Do you put a voodoo spell on them that make them fall in love with you, and then they can't let go?" She then said, "You need to tell me what it is, so I can do it." LOL.

Honestly I don't know what to do. I would rather be alone and forget about everything and everyone. That would be so much easier, and I wouldn't have to break anyone's heart. I could do my own thing and just be happy, but life is difficult. I don't know why Eric is still holding on. He has a girlfriend, and we have not done anything for, like, two years. John is hanging on for the fact I led him on so that's my fault, and my husband, Scott, says he wants to try and make it work, or at least help me make the right choices. What am I going to do?

Feb. 14, 2011

Today's Valentine's Day, and I'm at work. Me and John were talking, and My knows my concern with John and decided it would help if she told John in a way that seemed like she was curious, and so I found out a little more on how he feels and what would happen if I moved in and if it didn't work out. He cares about me and then told me that I was playing with his heart and that I needed to make a decision. I bought him a rose and a card and drove them to his house, so he got it when he got home today. Completely took him by surprise.

I bought Scott a dozen roses and a card when I got to work today. He made dinner, and it went okay. No fighting yelling or any rude comments today. Turned out to be a nice evening. I want to be with John and also remain friends with Scott. I want his approval. It would be nice.

Feb. 21, 2011

So as I sit here before I go to work, I can't help but realize how I fucked up my life—and not just mine. I have fucked up my relationship with Scott and made promises to John, and I have lied and cheated on all my partners and destroyed their happiness.

This week, I am off Wednesday and Thursday, and so I am going to take myself out of this picture. I know, according to the books that I have been reading, that if one commits suicide, then they go back into Vito, in which you are forced to be reborn and relive your life and your supposed to make different choices and correct the behavior or you must do it all over again till you do it right. Something Silva Brown writes in her books about the afterlife or something like that, and they relive their life over again. I don't care. I just hope that next time, I am born with the ability to be a person who does not fuck up everyone's life, who can sleep with one person and only one, and who doesn't hurt everyone like I have done in this life.

So my plan is to take a bunch of pills and have some alcohol, and we will see from there. I don't know if I could actually cut my wrist. I was kind of hoping Scott had a small gun that would do the trick, but all he has is a shotgun, and there is no way I could use it on myself, although time will tell. Who knows?

Mar. 2, 2011

Well, as you guessed it, I am still around. My plan didn't work. On Wednesday, I was going to go through with my plan, but Scott and I got into a fight after we got home from the casino. He didn't want to listen to this song, and so I called him an ass, and he got mad, so that led to more fighting and yelling. While we were eating, I got frustrated, and so I just threw my food away and went outside to smoke. Well, he comes running out, grabs my hand, takes the cigarette, and throws it, so I turned and walked to the bedroom. Well, he continued to follow, and so I get up to go to the couch, and he grabs ahold of me and won't let me go. I finally get away and go into the living room. He comes out and grabs the blanket off me and keeps yelling, then he tries to pick me up. So my plan didn't work out as planned.

Then on Saturday, we are at the casino and actually having a good time when he brings up the fact that I have no friends and that it is my fault and that I have caused all my problems. In a way, he might be right, but I started to cry a little bit. Then I found out after him telling me not to tell anyone about what's going on that he told his kids, so now they are not talking to me, which makes me feel uncomfortable when they are here. This makes me mad because he asked me not to tell anyone that we both talk to on a regular basis, but he goes and tells the daughter who still lives here with us? This makes me upset, and I miss my friend. I want to text him, but I need to let him move on and not wait for me because I don't want to be around anymore, and if he can move on, it would make things easier. I am off the next two days. Let's hope it works out for me. Let's pray it does.

Mar. 3, 2011

So last night, I thought it was the night. We were talking about me moving, and I took the pills and was feeling so drowsy that I went to sleep. I could hardly hold my head up, while Scott was telling me how I was a horrible person and how I ruined my life and all my friendships and relationships. I felt my heart rate drop. My breathing was so slow, and I could hardly move anything. I could see flashes of light. I got my hopes up and then eventually passed out.

But this morning, I woke up, so I went to breakfast. Scott is out riding bikes, and I feel a little drowsy still, so I stayed and took more pills mixed with some vodka, and I hope this will do the trick. I hope so with all my heart. It will be much easier for everyone involved, but the thing that worries me is after I drank the vodka, I threw up. I am hoping that I didn't throw up the pills. That would suck, but Scott knew something was up last night, and he moved the Vicodin from the cupboard and asked me if I had popped pills last night. I told him no, just the Tylenol. He knew I was lying because he removed all the pills and flushed them down the toilet this morning.

Apr. 6, 2011

Well, Shawn has not called me yet, so maybe he is not interested. My sister and her husband were joking around, and they both know that I like the bartender from the casino, and so my brother-in-law tries to be all sneaky, and I asked if they would give him my number. Travis agrees, and while we were ordering drinks, he slips Shawn a piece of paper with my cell number on it. Scott and I won't be going out for a while. We need to save some money and get some bills paid off. I can't wait for the day when I can be free and not be afraid of starting an argument or just dealing with the negative comments and added stress.

My birthday is in a few weeks, I will be on vacation, and who knows if it will be a repeat of last time. I went out even though we are getting along; I just don't feel anything for him. After everything that was said and done, I don't see it happening. I want to start a life. I am tired of hiding and drinking to deal with the fact that my life sucks and I won't ever be happy again. Have to go to work. Bye and enjoy.

Apr. 11, 2011

So this morning, I woke up, and there was a text on my phone from John. It reads, "Good morning, sunshine, I have been thinking. You should move in right away. I promise to take care of you and not just throw you out. The sooner we start our lives together, the sooner we could have kids. I am running out of time. I do love you and want to spend my life with you."

I don't know what to do, or when. Tonight we are going to the casino, and I got a text from John asking if I got his last text message and to at least acknowledge that I got it, so I told him, "Yeah, I got it, and it made me think."

Then I am sitting at the casino looking at Shawn, the bartender who works here, and I realized that he is most likely not interested. Don't know if it's because I still live with Scott or if he is just not interested.

Apr. 12, 2011

So I've been doing good lately. Haven't thought about hurting myself for some time now. But the last couple days, it has been weighing heavily on my mind. The text messages I got yesterday did not help one single bit. It made me sad, and I wanted to cry. I don't know what to do. John is willing to give me what I want, but I don't have the courage to do anything or to leave Scott. Scott does not like John, and I am so far in the hole with my bills, and the casino brings me peace and mind. I can drink and be happy, and there is no fighting, yelling, or disgusted looks. Well, going to sleep before work tonight. Enjoy

Apr. 28, 2011

Well, it's one in the morning, and I'm lying here trying to sleep and can't help but cry. What is wrong with me? Scott and I don't talk. There is no intimacy, and it is entirely my fault. We had the talk again on the twenty-sixth after we got home from the casino because I guess I was drinking too much and started flirting with Shawn. Scott said I am just a stupid girl and that anyone with any class would not be interested. He said I am so unhappy on the inside that I try and drink to make it go away and forget for a time that I am so sad, hurting, or unhappy. He also said I definitely would do well with help, with talking to a therapist or something. He said he doesn't want to live like this, that he is tired of me using him for a place to stay, that I take advantage of him for the cooking because I don't do much around the house. He also said that he doesn't want to be on suicide watch anymore, that he knows I have taken pills and or whatever.

What I want is to rent a place and figure my shit out. Do I really want to be with someone else? Do I really want out of this relationship? Or is the feeling that I have just an itch that I need to somehow scratch? Did I really rush into this house, or is this what I want? Well, I cannot figure this out being here, and going to John's will not help either. I need to be by myself. Time to cry and sort through my fucked up life at twenty-five. I never thought my life would be like this. Every time, I think I am doing the right thing or the thing that is best for everyone, someone always gets hurt or I turn out doing the complete opposite if what I wanted to do.

Apr. 29, 2011

So once again, I sit here at 12:30 a.m., going to bed after doing yard work and sitting around the house on my vacation. What a vacation! Tomorrow we have big plans, though—watch another movie and then go to Costco, yeah! What ever, I am going to the casino for some drinks. I don't care if he comes along or not. It is my vacation because before you know it, it is back to work. I want a life;

I want to know there just has to be. Well, good night and welcome to my crazy, fucked-up life, where everyone else seems happy and gets what they want but me.

May 7, 2011

Getting ready for work. Yesterday I texted John and told him that I would not be going over there anymore because it just keeps giving him the idea that we are going to be together. Told him it was not fair to him and that I needed to get my life together and that until I do, we are not going to do anything. He then wrote back, saying he is not hoping for anything and that he just wants to go back to friends with benefits like before, which will not work, in my opinion. I like the idea, but we both know how each other feels, and there is no hiding that.

Not going to the casino for a while because I need to save money, and seeing Shawn and knowing what he said makes it hard to enjoy myself. He said it's awkward because Scott's there with me and that he knows him. That's why he doesn't call or text. Not sure if that's true or if he's saying it to be nice, but it's not awkward talking to him, which surprises me. I thought after that it would be weird, but it is still nice. So hopefully, not going for a while will help me not think about him. So far, it has not worked out. I think about him and John. I think about how I ruined my marriage and how I want to have sex with my husband, but after we do and we get into a discussion, he always brings it up—that I am stupid and don't take things seriously—so I just keep myself from doing it.

I am tired of the stress at home, at work—everywhere I go. Scott says that my life is the way it is because of the things I do, that it is my fault I got molested when I was little and the things Buddy or Mat did. He tells me I'm the reason why I have no friends, why we fight, and why my sister and I don't keep in touch. Well, the reason I have no friends is because he never wants to let me go by myself to go and see them. He discourages every connection I have with anybody, especially if they are males. I wish I could just pack and leave, tell no one where I am going and start over—new life, new friends, new job, new everything—somewhere no one knows me or my past.

June 1, 2011

So tonight is Wednesday night. On Sunday, Scott and I got to talking. First, let me start over. After work, I mentioned going to the casino, and Scott said no, so then I went and took a nap, got up from that, and he wanted to barbecue and kept asking if I was going to drink anything. I kept saying no, and then finally I gave in. Then after a couple of drinks, he starts in with, "What's wrong with you?"

I told him, "Nothing."

He said, "What, are you mad that we didn't go to the casino?" Told him no, then he says, "You texted John like forty times on Thursday when you were watching the kids and I was running errands."

So I said, "What, you pulled the phone records?"

He says, "Yeah, and you called him."

I said, "We were talking about work, and he told me that Kurt, our assistant store manager, was leaving for like a month and so on. We only talked about work and the kids I was watching."

Then on top of that, he says, "You went and saw John today [Sunday]."

So I said, "What are you talking about?"

He said, "I check the miles on your car when you do overnighters or when you go early." He goes, "You drove like five extra miles today, so I know you went and saw him."

So I started laughing. Told him he sounded like my stepdad and that he had way too much time on his hands.

So then he messed up. He goes and brings up information that he would only know if he read this. He goes, "I know you gave Shawn your number. What makes you think he is going to call? He has class, and you're just a stupid, messed up girl, and I told you that you couldn't stay here and pursue another relationship."

So I said, "What makes you think I gave him my number?" I told him I didn't. I was telling the truth. It was Travis who did it.

Then he says, "Shawn told me what you did because he has class." Then he brings up, "Well, I know you fucked John and New Year's Eve."

Well, the only two people who know that is me and John, and I know he didn't say anything to him. He then went on to demanding why I was still there, so I told him I was waiting for him to tell me to leave, so he did.

I told him I would be out this weekend because I was supposed to watch my sister's kids Thursday and Friday.

He said, "No, you leave now."

So I packed up as much as I could and left. I texted Denise from the casino. Told her I was going up there because Scott and I had split, but to my surprise, she was working for Shawn because the week earlier, he'd twisted his ankle. She bought me a drink, and I really didn't want to go to John's, but I had to work the next day and didn't want to drive back and forth so often. I went to the casino and tried to invite some friends to hang out, but no one wanted to come, so I had a couple drinks and left. Denise saw me when I got there and asked where Scott was. I told her we were on a break but that we were going to remain friends.

So when I left Scott's house, he was crying, and I felt bad because I don't want him to be in pain. I want him to move on. I went to John's Monday after work, and for dinner we went to Applebee's. But Scott and I went there for drinks once, and it just reminded me of that time when we were happy and getting along, so then I got sad. Couldn't sleep much that night. Got up and went to work Tuesday. Didn't tell anyone about Scott and me. Since I had to be back to work that night, I went to John's to sleep since he was still working. Got about a two-hour nap and then was up. Had to work that night.

Then Wednesday, I needed to clean my uncle's house, so met up with Scott. We took a nap. It was nice. Slept from like 8:00 a.m. to 1:00 p.m. Cleaned and then had to go to Target. As I left Scott's to meet up with John because we had plans, I felt sad again. I noticed Scott was starting to cry, and he turned from me and walked away quickly. Luckily, he couldn't tell I was crying because of my sunglasses. I don't know what I am doing. I love my husband. I just hate how he is. John and I really don't know each other, and I hate change. How can I just throw away seven and a half years of histonry? I want to stay friends, if nothing else. The main reason is I just want a kid, and I would love for Scott and me to raise it, but I don't think that would ever happen. I miss Scott when I am not with him; I miss his friendship and the way he jokes about things. I don't know anything about John. I know the sex is good, but I really don't want to waste my time on trying to change someone who is set in his ways already. Maybe I am looking in the wrong places. I know the problems with Scott are from me. I cheated, I lied, and he will never get over that. He will never like John, and I don't even know where to begin on finding someone who will treat me right, who will love me, and who I will love and care for.

June 10, 2011

It's getting a little better being away from Scott, but now he keeps texting me or calling me to see when I will be coming over. He is always trying to get me to stay the night and hang out, but that is not making it easier on anybody; that is making it harder. I went by John's today to get my stuff. He was at work. I can't stay with him, so I packed up my stuff. Told him I can't do a relationship right now and that if he wants to stay friends with benefits, then we will see how that works. Then Jenn, Travis, and I went up to the casino, and, surprise, Shawn was working. I walked up, and Ernie was back and goes, "Hey, where is Scott?"

I told her that we were done, and Shawn overheard this, so then Shawn is talking to us quite a bit and tells me sorry for texting me one night about work. Guess he was drinking a lot when he was out for his ankle and decided to text me but deleted the number when I wrote back and said, "I think you have the wrong number." I didn't know who it was.

So then I tell Jenn and Travis. Travis takes a piece of paper, writes my number on it again, and hands it to him. Today at work, Jen, My, and I were all talking, and we all came up with the conclusion that it would be better to call it off with both guys and start over, and thats what I want to do.

June 20, 2011

It's Monday night. I don't have to work till midnight tomorrow. My sister is at work, and Travis and the kids are about to get ready for bed. I really don't have any extra money, but I want to go to the casino and see Shawn, so I go. I get there, and Shawn asked if I wrote the note to him with my number. Told him no, Travis did, and he goes, "That's what I thought," and I said, "It was just the number, right?"

He says, "No, Travis wrote on the bottom, 'I want you.'" He laughed and said, "Well, that worries me coming from a guy."

So then my sister calls, and I get a text while talking to her. I get off the phone, and I was like, "I just got a text from an unknown number." I look up, and Shawn is laughing. I said, "Was that you?" So then we are talking back and forth all night, and then he gets off like forty-five minutes early. I texted him and asked if he was coming back out, and he said, "Yep," so I waited. The bar closes, and I am walking out to my car, and I thought Shawn had gone home. I get a text on my phone, and it says, "What you doing tonight? Are you going home?"

I write back and said, "I guess. I have no plans," and then he says, "Well, do you want company?"

At this time, JJ, a bar waiter, sees me and stops. We get to talking, and he wants to know what I am doing. I finally get Shawn directions to where we are, and the three of us are outside. Well, Shawn says, "I have my boy and mom at my house," JJ says he has his wife and kids, and I tell them there is no one in my house. So they both agree to follow me home. We get there. Travis and Jen come over, and we all start talking. Then it's about 5:00 a.m., and the sun is coming up. JJ says he has to go, Jen and Travis go into their house, and I walk the guys out. JJ gets into his car and takes off. As I am saying "bye" to Shawn, he leans over and kisses me, and then we start kissing and ended up back in my room. Then it's about 6:00 a.m., and he was all like, ", I got to go. My boy is going to be waking up soon, and I am not going to get any sleep."

So then the day drags out, and it's about 1:00 p.m., and Shawn texted me again. He asked how I was feeling, and we get to talking and then again last night while I was at work. So when I got off work, I did not text him. I don't want to be a pest. He probably does not know how long I will sleep, and I want him to be able to spend time with his son while he is up and it's his day off. But Friday, we plan on going to the casino, and tonight I am going to by a new bed because my bed is a twin bunk, and it squeaks and is uncomfortable, and there is no room for two people. Scott is going with me but thinks I just want it because the one I got is too small. Then I am going to text Shawn and ask if he wants to help break it in.

June 16, 2011

So today I got my new bed and some blankets for it. I now owe an extra thousand dollars, so I guess during the next few months, I will be paying off more bills than saving, but in the long run, I will get the bills paid off and then start saving again. Scott is with me, and he is actually entertaining the kids, so that is nice. Now they both are arguing because Scott is hot and Nick still wants to play. I have not texted Shawn or anything. I want to wait till Scott is not with me and I can actually talk to him and not be rude. But tomorrow, I think we are all going over there, and so I will see him tomorrow.

June 17, 2011

It's Friday night, and I am off to the casino, but Shawn is not there and still no text. Maybe I had a one-night stand. It's weird, though, because I normally am the one who doesn't call the guys back. LOL. Oh well, guess it comes around to us all eventually. Ended up talking with Denise and guess she and her man Rich got into to it. She is tired that he does not pay any bills or work, and I guess he can't get it up all that often, so Ernie and Denise and JJ were all talking, and I called it in early and went home.

June 18, 2011

Today is Saturday, and I was an hour and a half late to work. Just overslept and didn't hear the alarm. Well, Jenn and Travis want to go to the casino tonight, but I have to work at 3:00 a.m. and don't know if Shawn will be there or if he is taking tonight off too to be with his kid. So I was telling my sister that he didn't work yesterday and that he has not texted me since Tuesday night and that I was worried it was only a one-night stand. Since I had to work all day, I went to lunch. Well, about fifteen minutes before I was off, I got a text from Shawn. "Hey, just coming down the hill. Was not too far from the Big Sandy. Sorry had no reception till now."

Well, whether that is true or not, at least he texted because I was done texting him at this point, LOL.

So we went to the casino, and it was busy, like it is every Saturday (and that is why I stopped going on Saturdays). Shawn was there, so I ended up closing the bar down and was talking with Shawn, Corey, and Denise all night. It was fun, but no sleep for me. I texted Shawn and asked if he wanted to come over and have some fun, but he called back and said he needed to get his kid and get to bed so he can spend time with him before he leaves, so I texted him and said, "Okay, let me know when your son leaves," and I am leaving it at that. We will see if he texts or anything. I don't want to be that girl you regret giving your number to, so we will let him make the next move. The ball is in his court.

June 19, 2011

So today is Father's Day, and I worked. Have not slept from the day before, and after work, I am planning on going to Scott's for a nap. Then we are heading down to his parents' house, which should be a blast, only because his kids know about us, and one of his daughters who is just as opinionated about everything decides she is not going to talk to me anymore. Guess she thinks she is an angel, and she does nothing wrong, but whatever, I don't care. The other daughter Erika still came up and gave me a hug and whatnot. We talked for a little bit, but the whole thing was just awkward. Texted Shawn once just to wish him a happy Father's Day, and he wrote back and said, "Thanks, hun," and I left it at that. I will no longer be texting him first, and I will not ask if he wants to have sex anymore. I am done with that. It's on him now.

June 20, 2011

Went to work, and then went and saw my stepdad. I guess Jenn told Stacy that I was living with her, and so now they all know, which is great. Scott didn't want them to know, but we'll see what happens. When I am bored, I miss my husband's company. Although we never did anything, I still miss him, and I still love him. It just didn't work out, and I don't think it will. I think I grew up so fast that I didn't get to be young and go out drinking and have fun. I didn't get to be a kid or a young adult. I didn't get the chance to date and see what's out there. I picked the first man who promised me the world and went with it. I promised not to break his heart, and about five years into the relationship, I did just that.

I am broke , and with so many bills, I won't be able to hit the casino till, like, Christmas just so I can get all these bills paid off.

I ordered Jenn a gas card with her name on it, and she said she will pay $150 every week, so I just hope I don't get screwed like last time. I really don't need this. We will see what happens. Baby is asleep, and I want to text Shawn so badly, but he works in a few hours, so he might be sleeping or getting ready. Who knows? I am very interested in seeing how this whole thing works out.

June 23, 2011

Was supposed to start my period on Tuesday, the twenty-first, and it's now Thursday and still no sign of it. I have taken two pregnancy tests, and both are negative. John is really waiting too, LOL. Scott also asked if I have had it. So yesterday, I was figuring out bills and thought that maybe if I could borrow one thousand dollars from Scott and pay him back till October, I can get ahead of these bills, so I texted him and asked. He told me to come down, and we would talk about it. So I went down there, and we ended up talking mostly about me and my problems and all the things I have been doing wrong for the last five years of my life. He then says he can't let me borrow the money and that I need to go to counseling and that he would pay for what my insurance doesn't cover, but he won't let me borrow anything.

I think counseling might help, but who knows? I will actually have to talk to someone. I texted Shawn briefly yesterday but have not been up to the casino since last Saturday night. I have no idea what, if anything, is going to take place. He might have been drunk and just wanted some, or he might actually be telling the truth about his son being up and spending time with him. Who knows?

I am tired of Scott calling me names. We're separated, and last night, he still called me a "lying, cheating slut and a prostitute" and said that I have so much hurt and anger inside of me and that I don't love myself and that if I can't even do that, then I can't love anyone else. He might be right, or maybe he's just trying to be mean, like always. I don't know what to do anymore. I just go through the days. They are all the same, and I have no one to talk to who won't judge me.

So just got out of the shower. It's about 7:41. I looked at my phone, and I had a text message. I just figured it was from Scott, and when I looked, it was from Shawn. I was so excited. I wrote him back, and it was about an hour and a half from when he wrote me and no response. This sucks, think I waited too long, then he texted me back late, and we wrote back and worth for a while.

June 25, 2011

So last night after leaving Scott's house, I drove up to the casino. I just wanted to see Shawn. When I walked up to the bar, he was not in there, and so I waited for Denise, but she had not seen me yet, so she didn't serve me. Then out of the corner of my eye, I saw Shawn, and he waved me over to a seat in front of him and started smiling. I was only planning on having like two drinks because I really didn't feel good, but I ended up staying until the bar closed and tried to get Shawn to come back with me, but he had to get up early, so it didn't work. He ended up calling me when he got home and said he wanted to come over tomorrow after work. The only thing that sucks with that is I have to work at six, but I'm going to sleep early and set an alarm and then stay awake and go to work. Although I am on my period, I can always give him a blow job and get him to finish, which I don't mind. Scott is mad at me because he thought I was staying the night last night and then thought I was coming back tonight because I had mentioned it, but that was before I knew I was going to have company. John also texted me because he wanted me to go with him tonight to go drinking and watch some game, but I decided against it, and I am waiting to see if Shawn is going to come over in a few hours.

June 26, 2011

It's 1:45 a.m., and I am waiting for Shawn to text me back to see what his plans are, if he is coming here or just going home. He might just be heading home, but I am waiting to make sure before I go back to sleep.

June 27, 2011

So yesterday, I went to work, and it was super slow, and I was only supposed to be there for four hours. I ended up leaving after three. I went to Scott's because I thought he still needed to get a battery for his car, but I guess his uncle came and helped him. Don't know if he told his uncle anything, and at this point, I don't care. I took a nap at his house and didn't have plans on staying the night after I found out I was supposed to watch the kids in the morning. Scott wanted to go eat which was fine, so we went to CPK, and then he was all, "Let's go bowling." Okay, that's fine. We get to the bowling alley, and there were legs going until eight, and it was only six, so then he mentions the casino. Told him that was fine even as I am thinking in the back of my head of how awkward it might be.

So then he says, "Oh, never mind because Shawn is working," like that matters, and then he just starts in with how I cheated on him with John, how we all went for drinks, how that was not cool, how I should not be in any relationship, and how I am a whore and a slut and this and that. I get mad. I can only take being called names so much until it's just irritating. So then I just stopped talking. Didn't want to do anything anymore. He was just pissing me off.

Then we head for his house, then I guess he realized he wanted ice cream, so we go to Baskin-Robbins, and he gets some. I am too mad to eat ice cream, so I don't get anything. He gets mad because I don't want ice cream, and we leave and go back to the bowling alley. He asked what I wanted to do, and I said, "Whatever, I don't care."

Then we get into a better mood and start drinking and playing. Everything was going good till I told him I was not staying the night, and then he goes, "Why?"

I said, "Because I have to watch the kids in the morning, and it would be easier, and then, I won't have to get up early, and I can sleep in."

He goes, "You have lost sleep over a guy before. What is the problem?" Then he goes, "What, are you expecting company?"

I told him, "I won't lie, but do not ask me a question you don't want to hear the answer to." I told him, "Well, I might text Shawn and see if he wants to come over."

That pissed him off. He was all like, "You're out with your husband, and we are having a good time, and then you are going to blow me off because you want to fuck some other guy?"

"Okay, first of all, let's clear this up. I don't want to be with you. You always put me down. You are so negative, and everything I do is wrong. You treat me like I am the lowest thing on earth, and you always bring up the past like it was yesterday."

So long story short, I went back to my sister's house, and I am not sure if he went up to the casino where Shawn was working like he mentioned. When I left, he only closed my door, not his, and Shawn didn't even mention that fact about coming over, so I am done texting Shawn and asking if he wants to do anything,

I sent him one last night and told him, "This is the last message I am sending. The offer is still good. You just let me know when."

I am done with all these guys. Forget all their stupid stuff, drama, and hateful comments. Scott is so dead set on me needing therapy because he thinks I will come running back into his arms for good, but there has been so much done and said, and that it is not going to happen.

Last night, he was sitting there, and he goes, "Oh my god, I just thought of something." It was so mean I can't even say it.

So I asked, "What?" and he goes, "The only person that wants to sleep with you is the one you don't want to sleep with."

I said, "Yeah, pretty much."

And he goes, "Oh, like when you were younger, your brother wanted to have sex with you, and you didn't want to sleep with him."

"Who the hell brings that shit up!"

Every time we have an argument or a disagreement, he always brings that painful memory up, and he wonders why I fuckin' hate him? Well, let me count the ways, you fuckin' dumbass. Then every time we get into an argument, he is always calling me names, and I don't understand it because if I wanted to, I could call him a limp-dick bastard or whatever, but there is no need for it. So at this point, I am not going to call or stop by, I am not going to text Shawn, and I am not going to John's. I am done, done with everything. It's pointless and a waste of my time.

Right now, I am so fuckin' broke I won't be going to the casino for a while, but that is fine with me. I just lose all my money when I go up there, and I only go so I can see Shawn, but there is no point in that anymore. I tried asking Scott for money, and then he said no, but he will pay for therapy. Then last night, he was all, "Well, we will see how much it is going to cost us," and I told him, "You mean, cost you? If I am paying, I am not going. That was not the deal."

I told him, "Yeah, I will go, but I am not paying," and he said he would. "What's this comment and remark about me paying for it? Forget that. I won't have money till December."

He looks at me and says, "Man, I don't even know how that must feel."

I was all, "What?"

He goes, "To have that much pain inside you."

"Look, I am getting through it just fine. Don't try and fix me. You might not like the outcome."

In all fairness, I think it could help or at least give me a better understanding of my life, but it is not going to make the two of us get back together. I can pretty much promise that. I fuckin' hate how he treats me, and right now I am enjoying my space and my freedom, and I don't need someone trying to be a father figure in my life. Forget him and his judgmental family. I am out.

Oh yeah, so Scott finally texted me back this morning, and I was just fuckin' around and asked, "Okay, where did you go last night?" and he goes, "Who told you I went anywhere?"

I said, "You just did."

He goes, "So I went to the casino."

And I said, "Are you kidding me?"

He goes, "No, Lilly was my bartender, and I only talked to Shawn like three times."

"Yeah, but what did you say?"

Guess Shawn got off at eleven and didn't talk or come by. Guess I lost that one. Oh well.

June 27, 2011

Okay, so last night, I went to the casino, and I did talk to Shawn. He actually called me before he got to work and basically said we are not going to be doing anything because I have too much stuff on my plate right now. Maybe later. He is probably right, so I then texted him and said, "We don't need a relationship, but we could do friends with benefits," and then added, "Okay, we don't even have to do the friends thing either." LOL.

Well, anyways, I was getting hit on all night, and I actually did not like it. It made me feel good a little, but then they wouldn't leave, and I was trying to get Shawn, so it was not helping. Then I decided that I didn't need to drive, so I texted Scott and asked him to pick me up and then headed to my car. Well, this guy who has been after me for a while was outside in the parking lot and followed me to my car and got it on the passenger side. Well, we ended up having sex in the parking lot at the casino while I was waiting for Scott. Don't think I will be going to the casino for a while, and I won't be texting Shawn for a while. I will give him a break and give myself time to think.

July 5, 2011

Today my girl Denis, who is a bartender up there as well, and I are meeting at the casino; it was a very bad day.

Thought I was going to get this loan and pay everything off, but that didn't happen. Then Travis had Jenn's keys, so we had to put the dog in my car, and that was just a mess. Katie and Tom met me at the casino, and then we hung out and had drinks. They left around twelve thirty. I stayed for another hour. and then I left. The bar was closed, and I thought Shawn had gone already, so I grabbed my stuff and left. By the time I get home, I get this message, and it asked if I left and if I was home. I said yes, and then Shawn says, "Oh, I was thinking about stopping by," so I told him, "Go ahead, you know where I live." So he came over, and we had sex, and then he needed to get home because his mom wanted to know where he was. She was watching his kid.

July 31, 2011

So I have not written in a couple days. Here it goes. Shawn has not come over since the day Katie and I showed up at the casino. He might have met me once but since I was texting and driving way too fast, I hit the curb, bent two of my rims, and blew two tires. I have been on vacation for a week and still have one more week to go. As far as I know, his son is either gone or leaving tomorrow. Have plans on going tonight but can't seem to get anyone to go with me. I hate going by myself because there is no one to talk to. I am hoping Shawn will come back with me tonight, but every time I hope that, it never happens, so, oh well, we will see.

Aug. 1, 2011

So last night went to the casino, and Denise was going to meet me there, and then later she texted me and told me she was drinking at her house and to stop by, so I asked Shawn if he was going, and after flirting all night, I left. A few hours later, he did indeed stop by, so we actually did sleep together, but he was having a difficult time because he had been drinking for a few hours. We ended up just calling it good and walked back out to where everyone was. It was kind of strange because I don't think anyone knew that he works with us. Well, I left before everyone, and it was about seven when I got home. I then invited him over a few times and, not to my surprise, really didn't get anything back.

I went to Scott's the next day. Shawn did call me one night when he got off work, which was on August 2, and told me he thinks it would be best if we didn't sleep together for a while because he likes Scott and thinks it is weird and does not want to hurt his feelings. Said he didn't text me back because he didn't know if I actually sent the message or if Scott did. Whatever. He should have thought about the last three times that we slept together. I am over it, and I won't be going to the casino for a while because I need to save up money and get things paid off. I just won't answer his drunken messages for a while and see where that goes. I like him a lot, but I don't really want to play these games either. I need to get these bills paid off before January, and there are things that I would like to do while I have money. I will let you know.

Aug. 10, 2011

So last night, I decided to go to the casino. I was talking with this lady and this guy about my ex-husband, and to my surprise, he shows up, just walks up right behind me. Talk about awkward. We then start arguing about this and that.

He wants to know why I don't have my rings on, and so then I go into telling him that we are never going to get back together and that he is wasting his time trying. I tell him that I don't care about being alone and that I am going to be the crazy old cat lady and that I don't need a man, and then before we both left, I told him that Shawn and I had slept together and that he was no longer interested because he wants to remain friends with Scott, and so then Scott tells me, "Well yeah, why would he want to be with you? He can have anybody he wants anybody who is prettier and thinner, and you're not something he wants."

That hurt a lot. It might be true. Who knows? I just don't care anymore. I am done with all the negative and hurtful comments. I texted Scott this morning and told him sorry for last night, and still he won't text me back. He is mad at me, and I think we are over.

Aug. 18, 2011

So last Sunday night on the fourteenth, I met up with Katie and her boyfriend, and then two of her old friends showed up as well. We got to drinking, and since I told Shawn that

I was not going to be begging him for sex anymore, I was not worried about anything. As the night was coming to an end, about 2:00 a.m., the one guy wanted to go because he had to work in the morning and he was not drinking, and anyways, by this time the bar was closed. I offered to drive Richard, the other guy who was there, home because he didn't want to leave just yet.

So we walk to my car, and we get in. Then he leans over and gives me a hard kiss, which is a turn-on for me. I like it a little rough. He then says, "Let's get a room."

I told him, "They're like $60."

He says he doesn't care, that he will pay for it, so we get out of the car and head back to the hotel part. Well, we find out that the cheapest one they have is like $120, so I told him I will drive, and so we walked back to the car. Then we made plans to go to a park and ride, and we would decide what to do there. We get to a park and ride and start making out. He is hard and tells me not to laugh because he thinks he is small.

Well, needless to say, he is not small, and he definitely knows how to work it. We fool around a little, and then he asks, "Well, can we go back to your place?"

I was like, "Yeah, let's go."

So we get back to my place, and he takes off his shoes and pants, and I never put mine back on. We make it to the bed and start going at it. He had never done it doggy style, and he had never had a blow job, and he was great because he was not used to one way. I could make him change things up. After a little while, I tried to take his shirt off, and he would not let me. Kept saying he was fat and that he didn't want it to come off. So we left it on for a while, and then I finally convinced him to take it off and said that we would turn the light off. So then we dozed off, or at least I did, and when I woke up, we were cuddling and then started to go back at it. He ended up finishing, and it was a good thing because I was getting sore , not to mention I still had to take him home and go to work.

While Richard was here, I did receive a text message from Shawn about 5:00 am. He asked how my night went, and I didn't even respond. I have made the decision not to go to the casino for a while because I need to save up my money and pay these bills off before January comes because my hours will get cut. The one thing I will miss about the casino is Shawn and the other bartenders. They are my friends, or at least act like it. I don't know.

So I am sitting here writing and texting Richard. He leaves tomorrow to go back to Washington, and he keeps texting me saying how I was amazing because I let him try new things and that I was wild, crazy, and good. He said I was the best he has ever had and that a lot of what we did was a first for him. That makes me feel good. Even if he is lying, it still makes me feel nice. I don't understand why Shawn, who I have slept with three separate times, could not even be interested since he is not even seeing anyone right now. You would think he could have fun and blow his load till he finds someone.

Aug. 22, 2011

So I am driving to Oakhurst, and Ray from work sends me a text and asked if I wanted to go to a movie. So I tell him, "Yeah, but it has to be like after eight because I have the kids," and he said that was fine. So I am running a little late, and as I am driving down to Fresno, I texted him like ten minutes till eight and asked if we were still on, and he said, "Yeah." He said that he was parked on top of the parking garage. I told him, "Wow, early."

He said, "Yeah, I don't get out much."

It turned out to be a fun night. No sex, and we went to dinner had a few drinks and then went back to his place for a movie and a couple more drinks. He then took me back to my car, and I went home around 2:30 a.m.

It was not too bad at work, a little awkward at first, but then we were talking a little. I asked him tonight if he wanted to go have a drink this week or something, and he told me he was busy all week and that he had his kids, so it would not happen.

Damn, I am horny, and I know I can go to John's and get it, or I could hit up Scott, but I don't want to go back down that road, so I sit here, and I hope that I can get Shawn here tonight. Probably won't happen, and I am going to be stuck doing it myself or, even worse, caving into John or Scott.

Sept. 2, 2011

So today I was looking at apartments online thinking about moving to Fresno just because I have been putting so many hours in at work and then coming up here and having the kids all evening. I am physically exhausted, and these kids don't listen, not to mention I get no time to myself. I can't just go out when I want because I am either watching the kids, or I need to pick them up from the bus or drop them off or something. It is really getting to me, and the question is, What did she do with them when I was not living here? She had other arrangements for them. It is not like I was always here. I want to start having fun. This is why I moved out of Scott's house—so I can do my own thing. I am kind of interested to see what Ray does next week, if he wants to go out or if maybe he is embarrassed about his weight. I don't know. All I do know is that today I was thinking about texting John and going over there.

Sept. 9, 2011

So I am sitting here with nothing to do. I work tomorrow, and it's my sisters first real day at Vons. I am no longer sleeping with John and Shawn. I guess he has a girlfriend now, so I am not even wasting my time texting him. Eric saw me yesterday at the Chevron and wants to know why the change in heart and how come I don't want to get together with him. Richard keeps texting me like ten-plus times a day, but he lives in Washington. It's nice to be wanted like that, but I am not doing the long-distance relationship, and I am afraid to even get back into one. I guess I can't ever be happy. I got what I wanted. I can do my own thing. I don't have to worry about checking in with Scott. but no matter how hard I work, I seem to never have any extra money. I have not been to the casino since the last time I went with Katie, and I have not been out since Ray and I went. I work forty-plus hours every given week, then have the kids on my days off. It pays my rent and helps my sister out, and so that is nice. I am just physically exhausted every day.

Tomorrow is a holiday, and with me working, I already have thirty-four hours for the week. I just need to pick up a few more, and then I can take two days off this week. That would be nice. I've been working six days a week for over a month now, and the checks are nice, keeping us from drowning. We should get the check from the jewelry on Tuesday, and I hope it's over a thousand dollars to help pay off some bills and household bills, so that will be exciting. My sister's job at Chevron told her they would work around schedule for the time being, so we are going to wait till she gets a couple of nice checks, and with mine, we are going to try to get that loan again. Hopefully we can get it this time, and then I am going to take three and give her three and get this stuff paid off. That would be awesome. I so hope we get it. I can pay off the gas card, Home Depot, Mor furniture for less, Best Buy, and depending on the amount we get on Tuesday, I could pay off Target and then work on paying the loan back. With me and Jenn paying it back, we can get it done a lot quicker. We could both send two hundred a month to it, and once it's paid off, turn around and do it again in a month or two.

Sept. 15, 2011

So I am constantly working and watching kids. I have no time to myself. I think it's starting to stress me out because I am not getting enough sleep, although I got my sister a job at Vons, and it's great. No one can tell us apart, and that's the best part. Ray still has not texted me or made any attempt to get together, Shawn keeps texting me, but he is really starting to irritate me. He texts me at, like, 4:00 a.m. when I am trying to sleep and then tells me he has met someone and this and that but still continues to text me. Like, about an hour ago, he is driving, and he texts me, "How are you?" Last Sunday, he texted and said that if he doesn't fall asleep, he was going to swing by my place at ten thirty, but I was at work…What is going on with this? You have a girlfriend or not, you want to be with me or not? Simply answer the question, no more games, please! Does it make him feel good telling me one thing and then the next day telling me something different? Tried for a loan today, and they are going to run my credit and see if I qualify. I hope so. I just want to get these bills paid, and then I can relax.

Sept. 25, 2011

So on the nineteenth, I went down and signed the papers for my loan. I got $5,000. I paid off Target, the gas bill, Best Buy, Bank of America, and Mor. Then today I bought a bedroom set for $400. Got it all moved in, and now I am sitting here thinking I still need to work my ass off to pay this loan back and be happy. I have nothing to keep me occupied except work and my sister, when she is home, and that is rare.

Sept. 26, 2011

So I think I have hit rock bottom. Let me tell you how the last week has gone. Now keep in mind I have been on my period. Last Sunday, as I was leaving the casino, I texted Shawn and asked if he wanted to come over, and to my surprise, he did. We had sex, and it was actually nice. He didn't stay, but it was on my bed, and he actually got undressed all the way. Anyways, then I went got the loan on Monday and then started my period on Wednesday morning. This week alone, I have heard three rumors about me at work, which kind of pisses me off, but here they go.

Monday, I was talking to John because I stopped by work to let my sister know I got the loan. I get accused of going to his house, which I didn't. Then on Tuesday morning, I get someone asking me about Ray asking another girl if I had a thing for him because of the way I say hi. Really? I have been saying hi like that for four years, and now people are going to think because I call him Ray Ray that we have something going on? Then I was on lunch Thursday night, and I get asked if I was fucking John because one of the girls from produce has heard that we were sleeping together.

Scott went to Santa Cruz Friday morning with his uncle till Sunday afternoon. This kind of makes me mad because now he wants to go all these places and do all these things, but when we were together, he didn't want to do or go anywhere. He always said we didn't have the money, or he didn't have time. I don't understand it. I just want to escape for a week and not tell anyone where I am or where I am going just disappear for a while.

Friday, I was at Scott's before I went to work, and he already left. I was listening to music and just started crying, I was thinking how my life is now and how I hurt him so bad and what I did. After I promised we would be together forever, I go and cheat on him and break his 'heart—badly too. It was not just once but constantly. Then I got made because he didn't trust me. I would not trust myself either. What was I thinking? So after I slept with Shawn on Sunday, I cried for like an hour on Friday. I texted John. I told him we are never going to happen, that it is not going to work and that he should just forget me. I went and got shit-faced at the bar in North Fork. I invited some guy I met at the casino the Friday before, and we ended up having sex.

Then Sunday, I bought a bedroom set and needed a truck to move it. Well, I was texting my friend Dustin, hoping he had a truck, and when I sent him the message, I sent it to Eric as well. Then he responds. He says yeah, he can help, but he does not get off till six, so I should let him know before that time if I still need him. So then he comes over, and we end up having sex, and it was good. However, he has a girlfriend, and he and I will never work out.

So then today, I am in Fresno, and I bought a shower kit to fix my shower and then realized that it would not fit in my trunk, so I have no options and nothing to do. It would not fit no matter what we did. So then the only person I could think of to call was John. After what I said to him Friday, I so did not want to call him and ask for his help. Then we ended up having sex. What I like about sleeping with him is that he lasts a long time. And then after we had sex, I jumped in the shower and then had the balls to text Ray and see what he was doing and if he wanted to have a drink or something. I tried to put a move on him.

What the heck am I doing? What am I thinking? I must have problems. John said we can be friends with benefits and asked when I was going to stop hating guys, when I would forgive. LOL. I told him I don't know. I don't forgive myself for what I did, so I don't think I deserve to be happy or in a relationship. I know for now I will not be asking Shawn to come over anymore. I will not be texting Ray or Dustin. Richard is far away, so I can still be friends with him but no more talking dirty or sending pictures. I will not be texting Eric, I will not be willing to run over to John's, and I will not be sleeping with Scott. I need to concentrate on myself, to try to make myself better and get ahold of myself. Don't think I will ever move on, though, until I can get over Scott or let him go. I hurt him so bad that I don't think I can let him go, at least not yet, even though he has been talking to a girl from work. I feel so guilty for what I did; I can't cut him out of my life.

Oct. 12, 2011

So I have been seeing this guy named Dustin, or should I say, I *was* seeing this guy. We have gotten together about once a week now for the last three weeks. Well, Friday night, he came over, and we ended up having drinks at my house with Jenn and Travis. We fooled around all night, then on Saturday, I went to work. On Sunday, I get this text from him saying, "You infected my penis with something."

I told him, "What?"

He said, "Yeah, it hurts to pee, and I am pissing blood."

Told him, "Well, you better go to the doctor's because I am pretty sure I have nothing."

Well, I don't hear from him for a couple of days, then he tells me on Tuesday that he went, and he is pretty sure I gave him chlamydia. I then asked him today when his doctor's appointment was, and he said he didn't have one, that he was going to wait for them to call him, and so I told him to call. He then tells me that he called, and they told him they would call back and that his phone was dying and that he didn't have his charger. He said that he would let me know as soon as possible. I think he is full of it, because you know how many things could reveal the same symptoms. Gallstones, kidney stones, bladder infection, urinary tract infection—the list goes on, but he jumps on the first STD they mention and then come out saying he doesn't know the people I have slept with and that he knows he got it from me because he has not slept with anyone in almost a year? Then when he was sitting in my house, he mentioned the last person he slept with and that was like a month and a half before me. He is lying, and he better not ask me to get together and do something because he has pissed me off.

Oct. 17, 2011

So I sit here on my day off wondering what I am going to do with the rest of my life. Am I really going to be living out of my sister's garage? Will I meet someone who is worth a damn, or should I figure out what to do with Scott? I love him, and I don't know what I would do if we were not still friends. I love being around him for the most part, but I hurt him so bad and broke his heart, and if we were to get back together, I don't know if I could actually say that I would not fall back into the same routine, that *we* would not fall into the same routine. I don't know what to do. I obviously can't be sleeping with several different guys because the thing with Dustin scared me enough that I don't really want to sleep with anyone. Then Shawn keeps texting me at all hours of the night saying he wants to come over and that he wants to know what I am doing or wearing. He wants to know what I am doing that next night or whatever. I can't do this. I told him not to worry about it, and then he says, "Well, I feel bad," and that he is not worried about it, but he is going to make it up to me and that I don't have a say in it that.

Dustin is completely out of the picture. I am not going to text him, and he has mentioned a Halloween party that I have known plans of going to. He has told me he likes me because I am a nice person and that he likes the way I am open and that I am a cool, pretty girl. Yeah, whatever, this was all before he got a UTI and then accused me of sleeping with all kinds of people and that I gave him chlamydia and that he doesn't know my past. Well, I don't know his either. We are not together anymore, and I am done with him and his stupid little games.

John and I don't really talk anymore, and I am not going to his house, and we are leaving things there—no sex and no talking about personal issues anymore.

I think about Scott and I feel guilty if I am out having fun with anyone else. I know he is talking to a girl from work, but I know they are not sleeping together because I know him, and I know that he is not like that. I feel bad because he is sitting around his house, and he doesn't really have a whole lot to keep him company or occupied. I get bored around the house, and I think about calling him all the time, but I fight it because I know I never will be able to fully move on until I let him go, till I get him out of my life and mind. I still worry about what he is doing or what he thinks, and when I am at his house, I feel awkward at times, and then I start falling back into the old routine. I get scared and run again, then we go back into the same thing.

Nov. 13, 2011

Okay, I have not written for a while, but here goes nothing. My brother Robert decided to send Jennifer, Nicole, and me a friend request on Facebook. Jennifer and Nicole accepted. As for me, I just left it alone. One day, I was getting ready for work, and he posted something on her wall, "Well, now we can stay in touch. Love you, sis."

I left it alone for a couple days, and then I couldn't do it anymore. I posted underneath it and said, "What makes you think she wants to stay in touch? That she actually wants to talk to you? Seriously, after all this time, what makes you think she cares about you?"

Then his wife posts, "Well, the phone goes both ways," and that she could have called, so then I wrote, "Yeah, like I said, she doesn't want to talk to him."

Then she writes back. She wants to know why I am so mad at her and wants to know what she did, so I tell her, "It's not what you did. It is what your husband did." She writes back and says, "He doesn't know what you are talking about."

So I sent him a message and said, "You really want to play with me? Because I will post it all over your page so your family and all your friends will see it."

This goes back and forth for a while, and she straight pisses me off, so I tell her what he did, and she refuses to believe me. Says I am lying just because I am mad and that I am fucked up for saying stuff like that when I am mad. She said that she'd wanted her kids to know where they come from—their aunts and stuff—but that the kids are better off thinking that their father was adopted because she is tired of the drama and fighting our family brings. I tell her, "Yeah, your kids are better thinking their dad was adopted and that she is lucky she had two boys and God didn't give her a girl."

So I go to write back, and she had blocked all messages from me. I tried to use Jenn's, and she did the same. I was mad, and I would be damned if she got the last word in, so I created a new account and sent her what I thought. Told her I don't care if she believes me or not, but I could go into great details about what he did and this and that. She never responded. She deleted her Facebook account, and he did the same, and I never heard from either one since. I told her about his little doctor-patient game and told her she could ask him about it. Needless to say he didn't respond, and she deleted everything as well.

Dec. 10, 2011

So I am sitting here thinking. John and I are back at it, and Scott pissed me off. A few days ago, he went and dropped Sam, one of the rottweiler puppies, off on the side of the road because he simply didn't want her anymore. He wouldn't give her to me, even though the day before he dropped her, I sent him a text saying I would take her. He told his brother that she got out, so I was mad and told him the truth, and then they wouldn't stop texting me about it, so then I made both his brother and Lynn who is a good friend of the family mad when I told them no, I am not getting repo because he knows where I live, and he will come get her, and I have other animals to worry about here, not just her. I said that he likes that one, and all he has to do is come here and pick her up when no one is home. Who knows what he would do with her as well, told them I was sorry but there was nothing I could do, and that I was sorry because he probably did it just to get back at me.

So today is Saturday night. On Monday, I start therapy at 3:00 p.m. I'm so nervous and not sure what to think. My sister and her husband are at the casino, and I think I might head up there. They have no kids with them, and maybe they will stay and have a drink with me. Who knows? I will see, hopefully.

Chapter 10

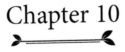

Jan. 16, 2012

So I have not written in a while. Ray and I went out to the movies, and we were talking here and there. It's Monday morning, and Friday, Jenn, Travis, and I get the keys to a rental in the Ranchos, and it is so much closer to work and Fresno that maybe I will have a life, go out, and have fun. Anyways last night, I got off of work and sent Ray a text. I asked what he was doing later, and he never wrote back, so then I sent him another message, and I asked so honestly, "Would you like me to leave you alone?" and he said yes.

I was a little sad because I thought that maybe something would come from that. I guess not. I understand he has a lot on his mind, but I thought that I could help him with that.

I went to therapy, and it was awesome. I loved it. Then the first of the year missed everything up, so I need to call and get it fixed if I plan on going back. I think it would help. My therapist said she admires me and that I probably cheated because I didn't want to be with him anymore and that a relationship should start with trust and then go from there, and since he doesn't trust me, he has his own issues with that. I told Matt, a coworker, last night that I was not interested in him because I have a girlfriend, and thinks he believed it. I don't care if it gets around work that I am a lesbian. Whatever.

Jan. 26, 2012

So Scott's dad is in the hospital again. He has been there for a couple weeks. It sucks to see him in so much pain and confusion. Then last night, Scott and I went to the hospital, and he had just gone to lunch with Margrie, this is the coworker of mine that he has been hanging around with. They went to Red Lobster, which is my favorite place. After the hospital, we went to eat, and so I texted Margrie and reminded her that it was his birthday today. So anyways she wanted to come and eat with us. I said that was fine, and she showed up. I got to see the man that I fell in love with those eight years ago. He was laughing and having a good time, the two of them telling stories and planning a breakfast date today. I have to keep telling myself that I cheated because I was looking for a way out, that I truly want him to be happy and if that is brought on by talking to Margrie, then I have to deal with it because I broke his heart and he doesn't love me anymore. I just don't understand how that fun, energetic person I fell in love with eight years ago could be so cold and mean even before I cheated, then you see him with someone else, and he is laughing and having a good time.

I broke up with John. I can't do it, I think mainly because I can't forgive myself for what I did. I took someone's heart and trust and destroyed it. I split with him and ruined a good man's heart. John might have been the innocent victim in all this as well, but since I used him to get back at my husband, I can't see myself with him.

Feb. 1, 2012

So today, we went and cleaned Lloyd's house, Scott and me, and it went well. He helped do the whole thing, and at the end, he asked what I wanted to do with the money. I told him I don't care, whatever he wants. So he said, "Well, let's put $30 in savings, and then you take $20 for gas, and we will use $10 for food." It was nice just hanging out with him today, no arguments and no discussions about what I am doing and when. It still breaks my heart, and I still cry when I think about that part of my life being over. I don't know why. I do love him, but I have caused so much hurt, and I am not in love with him, or anyone for that matter, but as a person, I do love him. I cannot cut him out completely, and I don't think I want to. He still helps me out if I need it, and he is generally a good person. I have to deal with the fact that he and Margrie are friends and that he texts her when I am with him and he does not share any of their conversations with me and that I do, on more times than

I care to mention, get stood up because they are together or they are texting, and he forgets to write me back. But he needs a life, and I want him to be happy, and she does it for him. Today they also moved his dad to a home, so I think it is only a matter of time before he goes, and that is sad because he is a sweet man in his own way and will definitely be missed. It's always hard to lose a parent at whatever age, and I feel for Scott and his dad. He does not want to really be here anymore. He is ready to leave.

Now with my personal life, I am pretty sure I am just done with guys in general. I can't seem to find anyone, and not that I am looking, but like I said, when I am out with someone, I feel guilt for all the stuff that I did to Scott when we were together. I thought the thing with Ray might have worked out well, at least for a little while, and he still tries to flirt and have fun at work, but I just ignore it. In all fairness, he asked me to stop texting him, and I understand that he has a lot going on right now with his ex-wife and his kids, but he didn't have to take it out on me. I was just trying to give him something to do. So I deleted his number and have not texted him since the day he asked me to stop; however, I still have his number saved in this computer, but that's as far as that goes.

I thought since I moved closer that Ray and I would hang out more, but we have not hung out since the move. I think I am just going to concentrate on getting my stuff paid off, working, and helping out with these kids. I don't need a man, and I don't need the drama I am over it. I really enjoy the girls' night with the people at work. They seem fun, and it gets my mind off the crazy stuff going on in my life right now. Well, that it for now. Good night, and hopefully the rest of my life will get better.

Feb. 27, 2012

So here goes nothing. My brother-in-law has a friend he works with. He thought it would be great if he introduced us and see where that would go, so he did he invited him over to work on his Jeep a couple of weeks ago. We started talking and had a great time. I thought that this could be it.

He came over a second time, and after everyone went to bed, we sat in the garage, and he said, "I don't want a relationship right now. I have a lot on my plate," and this and that. Mind you, we have been texting for a few days. So then he comes over on a Friday night with the intention of staying the night. We watch a few movies, and we're sitting on the couch, and I rub his back a little because he says he hurt it at work. He then asked about the toy that I have—I mentioned it—and he says, "Go get it." When I get back, he had his dick out, and so I begin sucking on it. We ended up in my bedroom and then later on the couch.

The next day, he goes to work and stays the night again. We have sex again in my room, and then he has to leave in the morning. He sends me like thirty messages a day, and I thought this was it, I'd found someone who I was attracted to and who likes me for me. I didn't meet him at the casino or when I was drunk. We had sex sober, and we still talk.

So today we were texting all day, and then I took a nap. I got up and showered, and he sends me a message saying he invited Travis to lunch, and Travis asked if we were dating, and he tells him no. Then he tells me Travis had asked if we were dating, and I asked what he said. He says, "I told him the truth. We are not dating and that we are just friends." That statement hurt so bad. I thought we had something. He makes me laugh, and I gave up men in general. I was doing so good. I'd stopped having sex with random people for random reasons. I wanted to find someone I could hang out with, someone who makes me feel important and makes me laugh. Guess I was wrong. I cried, and I think it's because I actually have feelings for this person, not to mention my ex is out with Margrie on a dinner date, and I have no one. Guess I am just not the dateable type. I really am getting tired of putting my heart out there and then getting it hurt; however, if I stopped sleeping with people in the first week of knowing them, this probably wouldn't happen.

Mar. 1, 2012

I'm sitting here alone, just thinking. I don't know why I can't ever find a nice, respectful person. Thought I'd found one, thought he could be the one. When I am with him, he makes me want to be a better person. He makes me laugh.

I don't want to be with anyone else other than him. I, for once in my life, gave up two hours of work just to come home because I knew he was here. He tries the lame excuse that since he is on probation, he does not want to hold me back from just picking up and going on vacation. Right. Like that's what I want or do. Whatever. So I figured if I lost weight and work on myself, then maybe I will be pretty for the next one.

Mar. 30, 2012

So it's my day off, and Jacob and I have been seeing each other for a few weeks now, and we don't talk about where the future is going to go or what we really are. I think he wants a friend with benefits, and that's all. I don't know how or when I got into this situation where I barely make enough to pay my bills, and it seems like I am never going to get ahead on anything. I work my ass off and get nowhere. I spend my days off watching kids and doing nothing. Scott won't sign the papers, and so I am currently stuck in this situation.

Apr. 4, 2012

So I sit here in my room. I just can't do it anymore. I don't want to. Between the kids and working six days a week and forty-plus hours, I still have no money, and I still can't afford to move out of my sister's house. I was doing okay when we lived in North Fork because it seemed liked I didn't watch the kids as much, or maybe I did, but now I am just getting burned out. I don't really have any true friends, no one I can just call up and hang out with or tell anything to. I guess that is life.

Jacob is supposed to be coming over for dinner. Have not really seen him since Saturday night. I got drunk and stood him up. We were supposed to go out to dinner and a movie, and I got scared and went to the pizza place and stayed there and got drunk. He was mad, and we have not really talked since, so I then told him that maybe we should just end this.

That was on Monday. Tuesday, he texted me back and said he didn't want to be done but would respect my wishes. He hopes I am happy, and he wishes me luck. The girls at work told me to try and work it out because they liked how happy I was with him. I just don't understand why I do this every time. When something is going good, I run, I tell them to leave me alone, or I pick a fight so we break up. So tonight, he will be here, and we will see how that goes. I just want to be happy and would love it if my life got just a little easier.

May 13, 2012

So I have been working nonstop for months now—six days, forty-plus hours—trying to pay stuff off, and I just can't seem to get ahead. Ray finally responded to a text message, and he says "You're asking me questions you already know the answers to. Just friends."

Well, at least I got an answer. Took a few months, but I got it. Scott has agreed to the sign the separation papers, and Margrie and I are getting along at work now. I came to the realization that maybe the reason why I was so mad at her and cared so much that the two of them were out is because I still cared about him and still have feelings.

Once I had a complete stranger tell me that, and I let him go. She does not drive me crazy. She told me a story that Scott finally got her cat to shake and that he now watches her cat when she was gone, and I didn't care. I am actually happy that he gets out and is happy. I really think the three of us can be friends.

Jacob broke up with me on Wednesday, and today is Sunday. Shawn and I have been writing lately, and he said something about meeting up with me tonight. I am not going to answer him if he asks. I don't want to go back there. I finally let that one alone. I am just so lonely. I have no one. Scott and I talk, but I try to not do anything with him because I feel so bad that I hurt him so much and that I don't want the feelings to come back. I want him to be happy, and I didn't do that for him. I hurt him, broke him, and lost his family, so I work and stay out of relationships. I don't want to hurt him or anyone else. I am just bored, and I want someone to like me for me and not because they see a piece of ass, which always seems to be the case when I meet someone.

I got drunk the other night and wrote Jacob and asked, "How come we can't be friends with benefits?" And he wrote back and said, "I thought you didn't want that," and I wrote back and said I would take that over the alternative. Now I am reconsidering that as well.

My sister and her family are at her mother-in-law's house, having dinner and a good old time. She asked if I wanted to go, but I declined. I don't like imposing, and I always feel uncomfortable when I am there. I need to get a handle on my life and everything in it. I still can't make ends meet, and I am working over forty hours a week. I just can't do it. I still owe so much to everything. I am still falling behind every week, and I am making more now than I have ever made.

So I am sitting here listening to music that just makes me lonely. I just need someone to make me laugh and take away my problems away just for a little. I just paid off one loan, and I think I want to take it out again so I have money, but I don't want to get stuck with the payments. I am going to try and wait, and hopefully Louise pays me back the $300 that I let him borrow, and then I will be fine, but I just hope it's next week and I don't have to keep asking for it.

I hope Scott is happy with where he is right now, and I hope one day he comes up to me and tells me he has found someone and he is happy and would like to get married. I just hope that day is soon.

June 4, 2012

Today is my day off. I actually have two this week, and I am still thinking of ways to pick up more hours. I have not started my period yet, and I am about two weeks late. I so hope I am pregnant. It would be the best thing that has happened to me in a long time. If I was, it would be Jacob's. There's also a very small possibility it's Scotts. Either way, I don't care. I would tell Scott it was not his, but I would let him claim the baby for taxes if he helped with day care while I was working and gave me one night a week to go out. I think he would be okay with that. I would not tell Jacob at all. He does not want kids, and I don't want him to think he has to help me with one. He told Travis the reason he didn't want to be with me is because I have too much drama in my life. I don't understand why he just couldn't tell me.

My brother-in-law gave his two-week notice at work, so maybe I will have more freedom, but I think this will cause a problem for me. It's going to lead to me paying something toward rent, I have a feeling. That was the reason I was not paying rent is because I was watching kids. Either way, I am not worried about it. If I was pregnant, my due date would be around February 2, and I would be having a baby boy. I am so excited. I hope I am. I would do everything I could for this baby—stop drinking and smoking, eat way better, exercise, and save for my son's future. I'd give him everything that I didn't have.

Later, I find out I'm not pregnant, so I moved and partied way too much with no cares. I have given up on planning and waiting

Aug. 27, 2012

So here goes nothing, I have not written in a long time, and I'm not even sure where I left off. So Friday, the twenty-fourth, I had a biopsy on my neck and am waiting for the results on that. This Friday, I have a consultation on my stomach, and hopefully that will be soon. I have been drinking way too much in these last few weeks, and two weeks ago, we went to Vegas. It was so much fun. My sister and a girl from work went just for the weekend. My brother-in-law wants me out more than he cares to let me know, and I have not been home but one night in two weeks. I don't want to go there. My sister is a slob, and so is her husband, and they have the hardest time keeping that house clean.

I have been hanging out at John's, which has been really nice. On Friday, after my biopsy, I went to Dominions, where I have been going a lot lately. Well, Jacob filled me in on that fact that we stopped seeing each other because he was seeing someone else, which really hurt my feelings because he lied to me again. Oh well.

So as I sat there waiting for John to get finished with whatever he was doing, I kept drinking. Well, this couple was there—they were always there—and they decided to come over and talk to me. It was about eleven thirty when I decided I was going to take off, and Maggie, the wife, asked if I wanted to go back to her house for some drinks.

I told her know that I had to go to my friend's house, and she kept insisting, so I decided I would go. I pull out of the parking lot and lose sight of the vehicle. At this point, I figure there is no point in looking for them, but as I start to leave for John's, they pull up next to me. She jumps out and rides with me. I then start to follow her husband, and I didn't think we had driven as far as we did. Long story short, the two of them wanted to have a threesome, and she thought I was cute and wanted me to participate. We ended up drinking more when we got back to their place, and I wanted to leave around 2:45 a.m.

Needless to say, as I was leaving the gate where I came in, the guard told me to use the gate on Valentine. I didn't know where that gate was, so I continued to drive around till I found a gate, and I assumed it was the one on Valentine. When I left, I tried to use the same directions as I did getting there. I made a left, then a right, crossed over the 99, which now was the wrong one. I thought it was the 168 and that I was in Clovis, and so I continued to drive, hoping I would find the 41 or something that looked familiar. I drove for what seemed like forever on a one-lane street with no street signs or any idea where I was headed. My gaslight came on, so now I was lost, had little to no gas, and my cell phone was dying. I looked for my wallet and then realized I didn't have that either.

It was like a horror movie, and I was the stupid girl who was going to run out of gas and have a dead battery, and no one knew where I was. I called John. He was not happy to hear what I had to say and told me he would deal with it in the morning. I was not happy, and so then I called Scott, and he just started yelling at me. I explained my phone was dying and that I was running out of gas, and he wanted me to just keeping driving. I was then getting upset, and so I just hung up the phone and was done with that. I just felt defeated, and since there was nothing I could do, I turned off the phone, locked the doors, took the keys out of the ignition, put the seat back, and went to sleep. More than an hour later, someone was knocking on my window. I opened my eyes, and John was standing at my door. He felt bad, so he came and saved me. I turned my phone on, and there was nothing from Scott. He didn't try calling back or even send a message. I then wrote him. I said I was home and still nothing. I could have been killed, kidnapped, or raped, and he would have never known.

Today John gave me an ultimatum—if I go back to the pizza place, then he is done with me for good. He said nothing good happens there, and he is right. Three weeks ago, when I was leaving, Carlos, a regular at the pizza place, who works right next door, was there again drinking. He asked for a ride home. I didn't want to give him one and then felt bad because he would have to call his wife back, so I agreed, but not before I texted a friend. I told him to meet me outside and talk to me because Carlos already thought we were going out, so I figured this would show him that someone knew I was taking him home and that we were together.

Long story short, I told Carlos to give me directions because I am bad with directions, and so he told me turn here and then up there. I said, "We are going to your house, right? Because I don't remember this way."

We ended up in a deserted parking lot. I was pissed. He reached over, shut my car off, and took the keys out. At this time, I had quickly sobered up and was not happy. I told him, "What happened on taking you straight home?" I said I was not doing this, and he said I wouldn't get my keys back unless I did. Carlos claimed he wanted me to see this view on the hill, so I get out and walk up this hill to see nothing. He pushed me to the ground and begins pulling my clothes off. I am there half naked on the ground with a big man holding me down. He pulls off my underwear and shoves his hand so hard between my legs and won't stop. I quickly had a flashback at my childhood and figured the only way out is to fight it. I pushed his hand out and closed my legs so hard they hurt. He then grabs me and turns me over as I am grabbing at everything, dirt, grass. I try to make it back to my car, and he climbs on my back. He tries to thrust his dick into me, and it don't go. I struggle for what seemed like days, and I hurt. I am getting nowhere quick. Luckily his phone goes off, and it's his wife. I get the keys from him and drive off, leaving him out there by himself. Let him figure out his own way home.

Also a month or two before this, I was taking him home again, and he wanted just one more drink, so we stop at the office and go inside. He won't keep his hands off me the whole time, so when he orders another, I tell him it's time to leave. We head out, and someone broke into my car, stole my phone, cigarettes, and some credit cards. Instantly mad, I then go a crossed the street to the gas station by smokes, and two cops get out of their car, so yes after drinking, I walked up to them and begin making a claim. Carlos was so mad he decided to sneak around the back and I guess walked home.

Then one other time, I took him home, and he tries to make out with me. I keep pushing him away, and he won't stop. I drop him off, and he has his belt undone, and so when he gets out, his shorts fall to his feet, and he pulls them up real quick, then tells his wife that I was putting the moves on him and that I undid his belt, so she goes without talking to me for like a month. Nothing good comes from that place. Nothing.

Aug. 28, 2012

So today I got off work and so desperately wanted to go to Dominions for a drink. I don't like this ultimatum, but I know it is what's best. That place gets me into trouble, and right now I need to save money and get bills caught up and paid off. I hope this Friday my sister gets a lot of money for Travis's school because she owes me like six hundred dollars, and with that, I would be pretty caught up and less stressed. We will see until then.

Aug. 27, 2012

Okay, well John and I had a falling-out. Basically I went to Dominions and met up with my sister, then Renee came over, and we were there for hours. Renee wanted to come back to my house. I told her I was staying at John's, so I was not going home. She then thought it would be a good idea to go with Maggie and her husband, so I told her she needed to pay attention because that last time, I got lost, and I have to work in the morning and so on. So we went. The four of us all had fun for a while, then we left. It was about midnight when she drove back, and I called John. I told him I was on my way, and he asked where I was coming from. I told him, "A friend's house," and he asked, "Before that?"

I said, "Dominions," and told him that he can yell at me in the morning because I was drunk and I had to work. I get to his house and climb up the stairs, and he tells me to sleep on the couch or in the other room. Really forget that. I have my own bed at my sister's, so I grab my clothes and what else I would need for work, and I leave. I forgot my work shoes, so I texted him and asked if I could swing by in the morning and get them, and he said, "Yeah, and after work, you can get the rest of your shit."

So after work, I go and get my stuff, and he said he was sad that I choose the pizza place over him and that he was keeping his word and that we were through.

So fine. That is that, although he keeps texting me and asking me to come over, and when he left for a couple of days, he asked if I would feed his dog and then asked if I would move back in. He told me I can move in, just no pizza place and no other guys. The thing is, I just want to be done I don't want to do this anymore. I don't want to be in a relationship with John, and I don't want a man telling me what I can and can't do. I don't want to go back down that road.

And then I get to my sister's house, and it's a mess. There's food and dishes everywhere, and they keep taking my stuff. First it was my fan, then my DVD player. They let their kids play in my room, and I don't want to be here either. I can't afford to move out on my own, and they are driving me nuts. They are always in my business, and I am tired of it. I could go stay with my ex, but then he is all up in my business, but in a completely different way. I don't know what I am going to do. I just need to hang on for a couple more months, and hopefully I can get stuff paid off and be in a better situation. Hopefully, Joanne comes through on the first because I am so behind on bills, it sucks.

Aug. 28, 2012

So I wrote John and told him I appreciated the help and that right now, I don't want a relationship and that I needed to stop all the craziness and stuff I was doing. I said that I think we would be okay being just friends, no sex. He writes back, "K." That was it.

So then I went and asked Scott if there was any way he could help me with the loans, and he did pay off one of them. He let me borrow $300. I was kind of hoping he would pay off two of them, but one is better than none, and it does help out a little. I just need to get the taxes done and Heather paid back, and I will feel a lot better. I am going to call the IRS on Monday and see if there is any way I can make smaller payments for the month of August instead of all of it due on the 15. We will see, and the thing that pisses me off most is I let someone borrow $300, the money I took out in April for the taxes. He said he would pay me back in a week, so I figured I would send it to them then. My mistake. And then I borrowed money from a close friend and am trying my hardest to pay her back when I said I would, which happens to be the end of next month. I really hope my aunt Joanne can loan us some money. That would be great, and if it's only 300 dollars, I would really put it to use. I could free up some money with that and get the taxes paid, as well as Heather.

I was so down earlier, a mix of irritation, frustration, anger, and depression. I could really use a beer or a gun right now, that would make me feel a little better, and I wanted to text John and ask if I could come over for a beer, but after I wrote him and told him we were through, I think I am the last person he wants to hear from today or for the next month.

So I am sitting in my room, and Travis is cleaning this nasty-ass house, finally. Let's see if they get to the bathroom. The kitchen looks better. I can't wait till I can move out of this pigpen, but I know owe Scott so much money that moving out will have to wait. Not to mention I have not paid and am not planning on paying any credit cards, so my credit score is going to hit rock bottom, and it's going to take a year just to bring that back up. Oh well, it's a learning process, and I have learned my lesson.

Oct. 1, 2012

So I just left my sister's house. I am stressed to the limit. She told me the other day that she was a cutter; she went into great details and actually made me cry. She gave me permission to go with her on Tuesday to her doctor's. She is going to have him up her meds. What hurt me the most is she never trusted me enough to tell me; she doesn't talk to me! She tells everyone else—her mother-in-law, a friend at work, and then me. Why, I thought we were closer than that. I don't understand. I thought we were friends. Well, I was talking to John. I needed someone to talk to so, we were texting. Travis was putting music on my phone and decided he was going to read my messages. He tells my sister about them.

So I told her, "Well, you can let him know that he got his wish. He wanted me out well. There you go."

ess it won't work. I wish life was easier, I wish I was not broke, I wish my mom was still around, and I wish I had e chance to be happy and have a kid and not so many dical bills. I wish everything was different.

v, 26, 2012

my sister likes to show up with these bruises, and they arly look like someone is beating her ass, although she es to tell me they are from this or that. It's all bullshit. hen my boss and supervisors and coworkers all ask me if husband is beating her, I tell them the same story she s me. She walked into a wall, or her son jumped on her whatever. She likes to run to Scott and tell him all the f I am doing and all the ways I am fucking up. She tells that she can't trust me and all this crap because of her ing. She thinks I told people, but they can clearly see the ks, not to mention she likes to tell people different stories. done. She doesn't pay me back, she doesn't talk to me more, and so on. She even told Scott that she wouldn't be rised if I wasn't sleeping with her husband. Really, I can't d that man, and I hate how he treats my sister. He would he last person on earth I would try and sleep with.

12, 2012

itting here waiting for my check to hit my back account use then tomorrow, I am going to have to take some

To have my sister look at me and be mad and say she doesn't want to talk to me put me over my limit. I can't take it. I have been doing good lately and not cut myself or thought about taking pills, but the last couple of days, that is all I have thought about—which way is quicker, what combination I need to take, and so on. I hope my sister can talk to JoAnne and hopefully borrow some money and at least help me out because I would be a lot less stressed if she could. I miss my sister, and I love her. I just wish she would have trusted me a little more. So I am sitting at Scott's house, and he is not here, but I am relaxing and texting my sister because she wants to know why I am mad at her. I told her I was not mad at her and that her husband has been trying to get rid of me for months, and now he has succeeded, and the fact that he is going through my stuff is out of the question. So to end this drama and the fact he doesn't want me around my sister and he pays the bills and they have kids together, I will make the decision easy on everyone and just leave.

Oct. 5, 2012

So I just got back to Scott's, and, yes, I have been staying here since my sister's husband and I can't get along. I sucked up my pride and went back, only to pay bills off. He let me borrow $300 to pay off one of my payday loans. The only thing is, I have to finish him, like, every couple of days. He wants a hand job, and that's, like, my payment for staying here. I feel like a prostitute. I have to do something. I am driving myself crazy. If I don't do something, I am going to be stuck in this downhill spiral. It is totally missing with my emotions, my health, and my sanity. My sister is doing better, I guess. She doesn't talk to me, so I don't know what is going on. I miss my life the way it was, and I can't believe the mess that I am in right now. I fucked up, and so now I must live with my consequences.

Oct. 10, 2012

So it's Wednesday, and on Friday, I will have two loans paid off, and by the end of this month, I should have my taxes paid and Heather paid back, along with two payday loans paid off. Then I can save for car insurance and start paying off other things, like the smaller of the bills, or start paying the bills in general. We will see first things first, though. Let's get this month over and people paid back. I honestly don't know how much longer I can live in this house before Scott and I kill each other. We are not meant to live under the same roof.

Oct. 15, 2012

The other day, my sister let me read a rundown on herself. It made me cry for the longest time. I already knew most of it, but to read it from someone else, I don't know. It just hurt and brought so many memories. She is getting her cutting

under control and is doing a little better. I didn't realize t all her cutting started up again after the family reunio guess when she gave our uncle a hug, he licked her ear whispered how he missed her and that. I guess the t summers that she lived with them, he was a handsy guy liked to touch her when she was trying to go to sleep how I wish I could knock him out or yell at my aun allowing that or for bringing him into our family. It i me so mad that I just want to kill him and scream for what he did. When my sister calls for money, he influence my aunt to help us out. It makes me sad couldn't protect her from that and that I didn't kne would have tried to do something to stop him or s from having to go there. My sister feels this world h up on her and that she can't trust anyone. Well, i she is kind of right. This world has not given us a nothing; it seems like one thing after another. She new car, and I hope they can make the payments credit up, and buy a house or whatever they want

As for me, I just seem so mad all the time. what, I just can't make myself care about anythi want to go out or do anything. I just go to wor come here and sleep and try to forget about i bills and all the ways I have fucked up my lif five years. I wish I could go back to last year an the bad choices I made, although if I wasn't in I am in now, I wouldn't have learned anythin

money out before Friday because I won't have enough to cover the two loans that are going to be going through. So lately I have been feeling really down or whatever you want to call it and started up old habits. I have the uncontrollable urge to get out the scissors and start cutting. Normally I can just go to sleep or take my mind off of it by going out. Well, due to the fact that I am broke and have no money and Scott was getting mad because I was going out, I have been home. Saturday night, I went out, and I could tell Scott was pissed and didn't really want me going anywhere, and then I started feeling bad and guilty and whatnot, and so on the drive over, I was able to put three long scratches on my wrist. Sunday after work, John noticed the marks, and I can see he was sad and hurt at the same time, like he was confused and wanted to change it all. Scott didn't notice till today, which is Wednesday, four days later.

So a blast from the past has started texting again, and I am not even sure what I want to do. I do want to know why the sudden change in character. We are friends again, I guess. Not sure for how long this time. Ray sure is a strange one. I just hope it doesn't lead to the whole awkward silence again.

I am going to be broke forever. This I have decided. I did get some of the credit cards on a payment plan, and there is only one bill left that I need to take care of, and that is the Chevron bill. So we will see where it ends up. I just need to make the payments and stop using the cards.

Dec. 13, 2012

I want to cut. I want to take pills. I want to feel something other than the hurt and disappointment that I have got myself into. I have hurt so many people and have gotten myself into situations. I can't seem to get out of this mess. Every time I get get close, I fuck it up somehow. I cut again today and a few days ago, and I want to do it again. I can't do this! *I need help!*

So, yes, I can't sleep, and, yes, I cut again. I burned "F.U." on my leg, wrote "hell" on my knee, burned a couple of marks on my arm, and put a nice mark on my hip. I did so well for so long. There are no pills here that I can take, so I have resorted back to cutting. I want to be happy, I want to be normal, and I want to find someone who loves me who I can love back the same way. Scott loved me but wouldn't let me breathe, and I hurt him way too bad to put him through that again. John loves me, but I fucked up my marriage to be with him so I can't do that again, and then that's it.

Dec. 17, 2012

So on Friday, the fourteenth, Ray and I were texting, and he was talking about wrapping presents and whatnot, and then said he was hungry, so I told him to go eat, and he invited me over. Not sure if he was serious, so I got dressed and went. I got there, and we were talking for a little bit, and then he asked if I wanted a drink to calm the nerves, and so we had one. We laid out the guidelines of our little FWB deal, and I told him not to get crazy and profess his feelings, and he told me not to tell anyone at work because he could lose his job. We agreed to see where it goes.

Once the ice was broken, we did end up having sex. It went really well. Although I tried texting him here and there, he does not respond to my messages. He will have his kids this weekend, so we agreed no texting when he has his babies, and so I have sent my last messages to him yesterday and no more until he at least writes me back. I don't know what he is up to, but I know he is dealing with the fact that he was raised differently, and he thinks he did something wrong because legally, we are both still married. We will see if that changes and how this plays out in the future.

So on to something else, my account is still in the negatives, and I really can't afford to take out another loan, so I am kind of just riding this one out. Saturday night, the pressure got really bad, and I pretty much fucked up my arm. I cut so many times on it, and with the burns, it looks pretty bad. There is no way to even make up a story on it, so I keep it covered and tell people I scratched it and don't want it to get infected. John is the only one who has seen what it looks like now. I just want all this hurt and pain to go away. I can't do anything with my life, and I am stuck in one lie after the other. Honestly, I wish I could just go to sleep one day and not wake up. I have dreams of pissing people off and hoping they come back with revenge and kill me. As I am driving, I think to myself about running off the road into a tree or going head-on into a big trunk. Every day it just keeps getting worse, and I thought I was getting ahead on my bills and my financial situation. I thought I was doing okay. I guess not.

Jim, my store manager, has seen the Band-Aids on my wrist and asked what happened, but everyone else who matters don't ask. Ray had seen them and asked if I like pain and then walked away. I need to let these marks heal and try focusing on my life. John gets sad when he sees a new Band-Aid or a new mark. He tries to make me feel better and wants to save me, and Scott just says I am stupid. He says I can't even do that right. I can't even cut deep enough to end his pain and misery, whatever that is supposed to mean. It just makes me want to cut deeper.

Dec. 21, 2012

So I have not cut in a few days, and today while I was at work, I realized why I sleep with so many people and why I still have not found the one I am completely happy with. I don't long for men, like Scott says, or to be loved. I long for that look in the other person's eye, the gentle touch of his hand on my body, the feeling of beauty, the look in their eyes as they slowly take their hand and rub across my leg, and the fact that at that moment, I feel beautiful. See, John has lost that look because he already knows he can have it; he has become more aggressive, more controlling, and angrier and wants things his way, I guess. Scott lost that look a long time ago. Now he just says I am fat or stupid or puts me down. I don't understand why any man would tell their girlfriend or wife that they are fat or ugly or stupid.

I figured it out, and I have decided that from now on that I am making my own decisions and will stress only about the important things and ignore the unimportant. When I am feeling stressed, I am going to run. I need to get back into shape and for my own reason, no one else's.

Dec. 27, 2012

Last night, I had Heather over, and then we got Brad over. It turned out to be a good evening. I did text Ray and told him that his name was Sam when I was talking about him and that I actually had feelings for him, so I don't know what is going to happen now. Oh yes, and yesterday, Scott got diagnosed with diabetes. Talking about life changes! And my stepdad had surgery to get his gallbladder removed. And now it's late, and Ray never wrote back. Guess I blew it with him too. This sucks!

Chapter 11

Jan. 10, 2013

So on New Year's Eve, I went to Ray's, and we just hung out and talked for a little while, and I played with the dog. No sex. Today he opened, and we didn't really plan to talk, not intentionally, but it just happened. I keep thinking about John and how I just don't want to hurt him, and I know he likes me and that I just won't be able to make him happy.

On New Year's Eve was the last time that I cut, but I'm getting more anxiety every day. The bills keep piling up, and I can't seem to keep enough money in my account. One day, I will get caught up, one day I will find someone who loves me, and one day soon, I hope my life will end. I will have a good check this week, and hopefully I can make my car payment. It will be late but still paid. I need to find a new location to cut if I choose to do that because my arm is looking pretty bad, and I am tired of making up excuses, and there are a few people who know the truth, so they keep looking at it for any new marks. I just can't be happy; I can't have that inner peace that I once had eight years ago. I am happy when I am out having a few beers and talking, but once I leave, the pain starts up again, and just the drive home makes me want to pull over and start cutting. It makes me want to wear loose pants or shorts so the legs are visible. I have even thought on occasion to just start cutting through the pants I have on, but since I can't afford new clothes and have very limited number of pants, I don't.

Eddie started texting the other day and invited me over, but I was working the night shift, so I couldn't. It would be nice to see him again. He was the only person who looked at me and said that I was attractive, and he couldn't believe that I was single or that I actually had a problem finding anyone. He is fun to talk to because he likes to say what he thinks whenever and doesn't lie or try to sugarcoat anything. He actually makes me feel important and pretty.

Scott has been doing better lately, and it worries me that he is being nicer to me and is trying to help me and have me talk more because he says it helps just a little to get it out, but I don't want him to think we are getting back together. He has been hanging with Debbie a lot more these days, and I hope she makes him happy. I even hope they will get together, and then I can have some peace of mind. Debbie is a good friend, and I know at one point she had feelings for him. Scott is a hypocrite and wouldn't date her because he says she looks old and judges her on her looks, but I think they would be good together. I know she tells me one thing and tells him something completely different, but she once told me, she can see how he is controlling and what not.

Jan. 13, 2013

So Scott and I fought again. John texted me, and I wrote him back, and he asked who it was. I said "Richard" just because I didn't want to hear it, then we get into this argument about him being a retard and this and that. So I just say, "Look, we are only still married because of the insurance, and that's it. You and I are not getting back together, and if you think that is going to stop me, then you're mistaken because that's not far and not going to happen."

Ray wont text me back, and John pissed me off.

Feb. 10, 2013

So it's been a while, and a lot has changed. I talked to Scott, and we agreed to stay friends, and I told him that I wanted to move in with John. John and I talked a few days before this, and he said that in, like, six months, we could have the bills paid off and that we would try to have a kid at whatever cost. That is one thing that I want, and I would do anything for a kid.

So I have been here two weeks and, like, four days. It's going okay. I really would like to go out, but John broke his foot last week so I understand why he can't. Between the Vicodin and the fact that his foot is broken in three places, we should save the money and pay things off. I am just hoping and praying that when they get their tax return, I get the $750 from my sister, and I could pay off at least one and a half loans and be so much more relaxed and happy and keep doing what I am doing and get the rest of this stuff paid. We will see. Going to grab a beer and see where I end up at.

Feb. 11, 2013

So today I learned that my stepdad put $68,000 into an IRA after my mom died when he got her life insurance money, which hurt like hell and made me so pissed, not because he was not entitled to that money but because he lied, and till this week, I went with it. You see, he received $100,000 for her death. He paid off the house and bills and tied up some loose ends. He also paid some of Pam's bills to get her out of trouble from her husband, who had killed himself. The thing that pisses me off is he swore to us kids that after paying that stuff off, he was out of money. He didn't help out with anything, and the fact is that he told my sister and me that we needed to get a job to pay for stuff that we may need for school. So not only was he taking the money we were getting from the state, which was $600 apiece for all three of us, he was also having us give him half our checks to pay for food, electricity, and so on. He would disappear for weeks, and one time, he was even gone for a month and a half. He didn't tell us he was leaving. He just one day never returned home. I just prayed he paid the bills and that the power wouldn't go off. Lucky for us he left the spare key and the car.

I remember being hungry and not having any groceries and my brother coming over and asking where dad was. I'd said, "Don't know. He has been gone a couple weeks," and so my brother gave me money to go buy food. I took the car, although I didn't have a driver's license, and drove to Oakhurst.

I am so mad because he could have stepped up and been the father that we needed. Instead, he had me take control of the family and make sure that my brother went to school, that there was food on the table, and that we were safe and taken care of. I sit here and think about it and think of the life I could have had. I could have been a teenager with no worries. I could have had a life, gone to college like I wanted. It's the butterfly effect. He got mad because one of his new granddaughters didn't have a jacket on. , I remember not having a jacket until I bought my own. I remember having to buy all my own graduation stuff, tampons, food, and school supplies. He sat there and said he was looking at cars for Ashley, his oldest granddaughter, and said he was having a hard time because he wanted something that was safe. Are you kidding me! Jenn and I had to buy our own car, and, yes, it was $1,200 and not in the best shape. It ended up almost killing us. The power steering locked up, and we had balled tires on it. We ended up in the hospital for two months.

I wanted a life that was free from fear, to be safe in an environment and to have a place I could call home, but instead, at sixteen, he kicked us out, brought his new wife home two weeks after my mom died, and brought her two grown-ass children in. He didn't want his kids anymore, so he kicked us out and brings two adults in who are more than capable of taking care of themselves. What I needed was someone to step up and take control of the family, to let me be a fifteen-year-old who was going to school and playing soccer and working during the summer. I didn't want to juggle raising my sister and my brother, to cook, clean, and make sure they were going to school and doing homework, to make sure they ate and had clean clothes. I lost all respect for the man that I called dad. I went two years without talking to him before, and I will go a lot longer now. I think what hurts me is when I left Scott in May, I had a hard time paying my bills so around November or December, and I went over there and asked if I could borrow $500 and that I would have him paid back in a month tops. He looked me in the eyes and told me he was completely out of money, that he was having a hard time paying the monthly bills on the house and that he was overdrawn in his account and had no way of helping me. I find out today that the money Stacy gets from the government in cash, which is $500, she gives to him, and he claims her youngest daughter on his taxes, not to mention he collects the interest off his IRA every month. Talk about having your heart broken.

My brother Chris looked at me and says, "Well, we learned from our past, and I will tell you what, if someone ever walked into my house and molested my little girl, I would torment and kill that person, and don't sit here and tell me that they didn't know." He said he was only two years older, but he'd figured it out. "You know two grown-ass adults had to have known something, but like the rest of our lives, they just covered it up and ignored it."

My brother saying that means he knows what happened, and it hurts that I couldn't hide it from him. My brother has been through hell and back, and I wish both my sister and my brother luck in everything they do. I wish I could take all there stress and hurt away, make their lives better somehow, make them happy, and help them so they can help their children.

Chapter 12

May 17, 2014

So here goes nothing. It's been almost two years since I wrote, and a lot has happened. I sold my laptop because I wanted the money and because it was all messed up. I bought a new one that didn't have a program to write on, which kind of sucked. Anyways, it didn't work out with Jen and Travis. I was paying way too much to help support her and her family because Travis quit his job, so then I bounced back and forth between Scott's and John's house.

John gave me a $3,000 loan to pay off some stuff, payday loans I had out, and to cover some taxes I owed. I did have a payment plan worked out on how I was going to pay him back; however, me living with him didn't work out either. We got into a fight, and so I went searching for an apartment.

I found one and moved in May 1, 2013. I also met a man around that time. His name is Ray, and he works at Ozzys, which is a bar and grill across from work (where the old red zone was). I first saw him at the end of February when I was out with Eddy. That was the last time that Eddy and I hooked up. I was on vacation and living with John and was already waiting for my apartment to be ready, so we were kind of celebrating. Then a few weeks later, I went back, and it was a slow night, and so I got to talking to the bartender for a few hours, and he kept pouring me drinks. When I tried to close out my tab for the second time, he didn't charge me for anything, and so I asked for a pen and wrote my number down on a napkin and gave it to him. I couldn't help but love his smile, and there was just something about him. The look in his face and his eyes, he kind of reminds me of someone who has had a lot of hurt and may be too afraid to trust or go down that road. I am living with Scott at this time, so Ray and I texted back and forth for a while. I really like him. He is forty-five, with two kids—one girl who is twenty-seven and a son, twenty-four, divorced.

So I moved into my apartment with the help of Scott and for the first few months was struggling like crazy. I was still repaying the loan back to John and was getting behind on my bills and drinking way too much and way too often. Katie graduated and came back home and was staying with her grandma and driving back and forth a good distance for work. I picked up a second job at Chevron again, then I started traveling for work, and Katie asked if I could use a roommate, and so I took her up on the offer. With help on rent and my second job, I was finally getting caught up on things, and my stress level finally went to normal. I was seeing Ray and making good on bills, and everything was going good. I was definitely working way too much, and although the money was good, I was slowly killing myself with lack of sleep and then oversleeping through alarms. I had to quit Chevron. Then Steve, a coworker, and I started hanging out outside of work, and we started going out for drinks on Fridays, and he started coming over, and, yes, we slept together for the first time in September around the first week.

Then two weeks later, I started jury duty and was there for three weeks and could not figure out why I was so tired. I was working all night and then doing jury duty during the day, but before, I had done two jobs and hadn't been this tired, I couldn't believe it. Keep in mind that I am still seeing Ray.

Since I was off my shots, that put me in menopause, and I did the whole spotting and finally had a month with a regular period. It was no surprise to me that in October, my period never came. I was so used to not having one or it being late and irregular that when my roommate happened to be on hers again, it made me question whether or not the treatment was going to work. So as I thought about maybe that, the possibility of being pregnant crossed my mind for a second. So the day was Halloween, and I bought a twelve-pack of beer and headed home. I took my nap after work and got up. Since I had to work that night and it was already late, I didn't drink anything, but then I remember that I did have a pregnancy test under the sink and thought, *Why not try it.* So I took the test and figured it was going to come back negative like so many times before. As I pee on the stick, it starts changing, and it looks like maybe I am pregnant, but I didn't want to get my hopes up, so I head outside for a smoke. I come back in, and to my surprise, I am pregnant. Now I definitely can't have that beer. I grab my phone, take a picture, and send it off to my sister, totally forgetting that it is Halloween night. I have her call our primary and set up an appointment for the following day to make sure because it was an old test. I headed into work and am so nervous. I don't want to do anything to harm my baby and definitely can't tell anyone. I am not even sure if I actually am pregnant, and if I am, I don't even know how far I am.

So I made it through work, went to primary with my sister, and, yes, it's confirmed. I am five weeks pregnant. So excited. Jen tells my brother and his wife but told her not to tell anyone else. It's still early, and I don't want anyone to know. I call my ob-gyn and set up an appointment, but with jury duty going from nine to five, Monday through Thursday, it's hard to find an opening, so I have to wait three weeks before I can get it. I finally get in, and they give me all kinds of information and set up an ultrasound to make sure baby is in the uterus. I got to see my eight-week-old baby, and I am so excited. I was doing really well.

I stopped drinking, cut way back on the caffeine and the smoking, and was being really careful. I then had to tell Steve and Ray. I sent Ray a text, and it simply read, "What would you say if I told you I was eight weeks pregnant." I got no response.

Steve was told a little differently. I waited till one Friday afternoon when he came over. After he left, I texted him and said, "Hey, wanted to tell you before it got out at work, I am pregnant, but don't worry, I am a month further along than when you and I have been seeing each other." Doubt he believed me, but I had to say something. He knows I wouldn't do anything to mess up his job or his marriage. So now both people know, but I have no clue whose kid it is. Steve is younger and a different race, not that it matters. My child will just always have a tan married. Ray is older and white and, as far as I know, doesn't want any more kids. They tend to move past that stage as they get older and already have some.

I go through the next five months not telling anyone anything. There is really only a handful of people who know, and as I approach the six-month mark, I go ahead and let the cat out of the bag. I don't care who knows. It seems to be going well. Then one day as I am driving, I get into a car accident. Some guy tries to make a left-hand turn and doesn't see my car. I am freaking out. I spent twelve hours in the ER labor and delivery to make sure the baby is okay, and then a couple of days later, they tell me I am in preterm labor, and I am taken out of work. I am crapping and spotting, and there is nothing they can do but hope he stays put. I am too early for any medication to make this baby live, so I am praying he holds on for me. I was placed on bed rest for a week, and then things started to get better. He was going to stay put, but they kept me out of work just to make sure.

So now I am starting my thirty-fifth week, and everything is good. I am having a boy, and the baby looks good. I have two to five weeks left, and although I am completely scared of messing his life up, I am equally happy. My roommate moved out because she doesn't want to get woken up when the baby cries, and she is not all that thrilled on me being pregnant. Ray and I don't really talk about the fact that I am pregnant, although it is clear since I can't hide the belly. We still talk, and last night, I was just over there, so we will see what happens when my baby boy is born.

Both guys know that I was seeing someone else and that they very well could be or not be the father. We will just have to wait and find out. I think it would be interesting to see what they do when he is born, but I have Scott and my brother, who both are willing to help me out once he is born, and so I think I am going to be okay. My wish for a baby finally came true, and I can't be more excited and scared shitless all at the same time. All I can do is wait and see and pray to God and give him all my gratitude for finally making my wish come true.

Although I am struggling with bills now because I was taken out of work way earlier than I expected, I am hoping I can get a good settlement, or at least something to help me get back on my feet. Not only am I not with the baby's daddy, I am not even sure who he is. In the following month, if I don't get my settlement check, I am going to have to call someone and ask for about $500 to cover the rent until I can get paid. My baby boy will be here by then, and all I have to do is see if the baby's dad steps up. I don't need him to continue to support him, but a little help for that month would be great—unless my money comes in.

My sister has not really been around. She has been running around with some boy she works with, and it makes me sad because I thought she would be more involved in my life now, especially because I am pregnant, and she of all people knows how excited I am, not to mention terrified.

Scott has been more than supportive in this whole thing. I just really hate having to go to all my appointments by myself. Although I have tried to get Scott to go to one, he has nicely declined. So I guess I am in this alone, just me and my baby boy, who I have decided to name after my brother and father-in-law. Christopher Jack Seymour will be here really soon, and I can't wait to meet my baby boy. Finally, after all these years of waiting and silently wishing, I finally got the one thing in this life that I couldn't or didn't want to go without.

May 22, 2014

So today I had a check with my doctor for the baby, and I am just ending thirty-five weeks. Everything was good, and I go back in two weeks. I can't wait till this baby comes because I will feel a whole better when he is out and in my arms. Once again I had to go by myself. Thought my sister would be there, but like normal, she forgot. I just want to meet my baby boy and to see what he is going to look like. This weekend, my aunt and uncle will be at my brothers, so I will be spending most of the weekend up there, and that will keep my mind off waiting around for his arrival. When I go back to my appointment, I will be starting thirty-eight weeks, and at that time, my baby will be considered full term, so any time after that would be good.

June 2, 2014

So last weekend, I spent Friday, Saturday, and Sunday at my brother's because my aunt came up. It was a lot of fun hanging out with family and catching up. Then Monday, I came down with these hives, which I thought was maybe because I got attacked by bugs or something, but I came to find out it's called PUPPP and is caused by being pregnant with a boy in the last trimester. The only way to get rid of it is delivery, which sucks because they itch like crazy, so I got into my doctors today, and she gave me a shot and some cream to see if it will help with the itching. She also checked my cervix and said I was almost two centimeters dilated, and so that means soon my little bug will be here. I am so excited. I can't wait to me him and to see what he is going to look like. I am hoping I can get him here with in the next week in a half, so this means lots of walking and motivation. We will see.

June 16, 2014

So I wait for my baby boy to arrive, and the anticipation is driving me crazy. The other day, John asked me what I was going to tell my son when he asked about his dad! Well, honestly, I will tell him the truth when he is older, when he can understand, and I will make sure that he understands that his momma messed up and that it was my mistake and no else. I want him to know that he was wanted and that he is loved, and I never want him to think that he was not wanted, not even for a second. I know I have made mistakes and that I am not perfect and that if I could do it over, I would only change one thing, and that would be to know and have his dad in his life because even up to this point, I myself don't even know who his daddy is. Once my baby boy is born, I plan on finding out, just so I can know, and so when the child does ask, I can honestly tell him who he was or is.

In all fairness, I do care about each one of the guys. Steve has a wife who he cares about, and I can't hold him responsible for my nonstop asking and for my ability to sleep with a married man. John I care about as a person, but I can't be with him for the simple fact we don't get along when we are together as a couple. Then there is Ray, who I really truly care about and so deeply wish is the father, although four months after telling him I was pregnant, I find out that he may be fixed. He says he doesn't know, and I am not sure how I am supposed to take that. I do understand that he is older and has raised his kids, and the last thing this man I am sure wants is a baby to raise. I plan on doing this on my own, though, with the help of my family, and my ex-husband, so far, says he is willing to help, and I am not sure why. Although I plan to try my best to give my son everything I didn't have and to make sure he is loved and well taken care of, I know it's going to be very difficult being a single mom and having to work full time to support him, but I am willing to do anything and everything for him. I just need him to come out so I can meet my baby boy face-to-face and so I can hold him in my arms for the first time. I can't wait.

Aug. 2, 2014,

So my baby boy arrived on June 29 2014. He was a healthy baby—6 pounds, 14.4 ounces—and he is the love of my life. I texted Ray the Thursday night before the weekend I had the baby, and then he went three weeks without talking to me. I finally wrote him and asked, "So if I didn't keep the baby, would you have stuck around?" and, of course, I got no response. Although to my surprise, last week he actually asked for my address and stopped by. I asked if he would do a DNA test just so when my son asks who his dad is, I can at least give him an answer, but I think that is going to be for my own personal use because I don't want to tell my son that his dad knew about him but chose not to be a part of his life. He said he would do it, and the next time he came over, we took the test, and I mailed it off, so next week, I should have the results mailed to me. So we will see.

I haven't talked to Steve in a while. I have no idea what he is thinking or if he even thinks this boy is his. I am so stressed right now. I haven't paid a credit card bill in a month, and right now, I am starting to get the second month, late fee, and still currently waiting on my settlement. I told Scott I would give him some, and I can't even get him to watch my kid longer than two hours to go out. He said he wouldn't do it. Thank God my sister is helping me out so much. She is loaning me money and watching my boy when she gets the night off. It's great. She knows I am waiting on that money and that I will pay her back as soon as I get it. She has even offered me to go live with her till I get caught back up, which I have thought about a lot tonight. At least for a couple of months, I would save at least $700 a month not paying rent PG&E and the TV. All I would have to do is pay for some groceries, which is not bad. John mentioned it but said he won't be a babysitter, which is fine, at least till I got caught up, so I am still thinking of that possibility too. We will see. Going to pay my rent and probably give my notice. I don't really want to, but I don't think I have a choice. I need to do something for my son. I can't be this stressed and try and raise a kid. It's not healthy for him, and it leaves me to make bad decisions when I am around sharp objects and when there are some pills near me. I can't leave my boy, but I can't raise him this way.

Aug. 12, 2014,

So the DNA test came back, and Ray was not the dad, so just out of thought, I decided to let John know and asked if I should tell the other person. He said no. My dad said I should tell him just so he knows, but I really don't want anything to make it clear. So tonight, I text John to see what he was up to, and he responded that he has a girlfriend now and doesn't want to mess that up. So I am thinking that maybe he didn't want to know if the baby was the other guy's simply because he doesn't it want to be his after all the lies and the broken promises on how we would try and have a kid and this and that. He doesn't want anything to do with me or my son. So I guess I need to finally let that be. I did write back and say "okay." I will respect his wish. It simply would never have worked out between us, and I should let him go so he can find someone who makes him happy because I honestly can never see myself with him. It does make me a little mad, because John had said over and over that we would try and do anything to have a kid, even go as far as adopting, so having someone else's kid was not a problem then! Why now?

Steve wrote the other day and asked if I wanted to go for drinks one of these days, and I guess I will mention it to him that this little boy has his eyes and nose. I have talked to Ray on occasion, and since he has a little interest in what I am doing, I don't know where this is going to go. I sent him a text saying how I felt, and he didn't actually respond to that but did want to meet up last Thursday.

I go back to work in six weeks, and I am trying my hardest to stay afloat here. Sister wants to get a place near the casino, and the commute wouldn't be bad, but I am only going to do it if it is going to save me money. I need to get caught up on stuff and make a better life for me and my son. I love him with every ounce of my life, and the only thing I would change is not doing this alone. I wish every day that it was Ray's baby, only because I think he would have wanted it to be and think he would have helped out when he could. But that is life and the road I am on, so I will just love my son and make sure I can do everything I know how to give him a life I didn't have and to never let anything happen to him. I don't want him to ever feel like he is a burden and never to feel like he was not wanted. I will love him till the day they lay me in the ground. Even if I am alone, I will do it with a smile and make sure he is happy and healthy. I have been slipping a little bit of information here and there to Ray about my past, and so far, there has been no judgment. We will see how much he can take before he runs away.

Sept. 17, 2014

So I sit here thinking about the last few weeks, and this is the rundown.

Sept. 23, 2014

So here it goes. I found out that Ray was sleeping with Hollie, who is my best friend's ex-girlfriend. I was so pissed because he lied to me and slept with, out of all the people in the world, a friend of mine. She has been at my house, held my baby boy, and she knew firsthand how I felt about him. I asked Ray why her and why he lied, and he just keeps coming back to, "Well, you kissed that guy out in the parking lot," and so I tell him, "Yes, you are right, I did, but according to Hollie, you two have been fucking for a week in a half." This was the end of last month. So extremely pissed off, I call him out on Facebook and then deleted the whole thing and blocked Hollie from my account. Ray also blocked me from his. This took place in the same week of me returning to work because my insurance has been dropped, and they won't pay me to be out any longer, so already frustrated and not sure what I am going to do with baby, I get all this other stress dropped on top of it. Then a couple of days later, Hollie and Vicki are having drinks and talking. Hollie decides she will drive Vicki home to her house and just stay the night since they both have to work in the morning. Well, they start arguing, and Hollie starts hitting Vicki. Hollie gets arrested, and Vicki went to the hospital. To this day, Hollie is still waiting to see what happens in jail and is waiting to see how long she gets, so karma does work out in the end.

Back to my current situation. I am going to have to move in with sister next month until I can get caught up on bills. Scott is loaning me the money to pay off my loans, which is going to be $3,200, and that will save me almost $900 a month. I probably could stay here and just live on a very tight budget, but I am tired of being stressed about money every week. The only way I could possibly stay here is if the baby daddy wanted to slip me money for the baby, I am talking like a couple hundred a month just to be on the safe side. I am planning on meeting him this week, and I wonder if he is going to ask about the baby. I don't want to tell him he has to do anything, and I don't really want to interfere with his life, but I would love it if he said, "Well, let me give you some money every week or month, and if I can, I would like to see him. I think it would be nice if my son had his dad in his life—even if it's only like a day or two a week."

As far as me seeing anyone, I have gotten close to my new grocery manager, Philip. We have had sex a couple times now, and I am not sure if he has actually finished or not. He seems to have a hard time keeping it hard, and I am not sure if he is just nervous when it comes to that or, like I mentioned, uncomfortable because it's only been about two weeks. He said he really likes that I am fun and that we have a lot in common and we think the same and what not. He is twenty-five and gets along with my son, which is nice, and he knows about the baby daddy and that it's his son. It's obvious since the baby looks just like him. So in the next few weeks, I need to make the decision on moving and start packing to move in with sister up in Oakhurst.

Chapter 13

Mar. 12, 2015

Okay, here we go again! So it's been a while, and in the last entry, I was contemplating a move to Oakhurst with Jenn, so, yes, I did move, and then a couple weeks after, we tried to make it work in a tiny two-bedroom upstairs apartment. It was going to be me and a newborn with her and her two kids on the days she got them and a coworker. It was going to work. I literally had everything I owned at Scott's house and only took two bags of clothes—one for me and one for the baby.

We then spent the next few weeks looking for a bigger place, at least three bedrooms. We then found a nice four-bedroom house for Jennifer and her two kids and Justice and Christopher and me. We moved in on her birthday, which was, like, the end of November, and things were going great. Then February comes, and Jennifer gets tired of Vons, not being able to see her babies, working to much, always being tired, and whatnot, so she quits. I support her decisions and told her I would help out, no problem.

Mar. 20, 2015

My sister came up to me and asked if Travis could move in. Claimed he would help pay her part of the bills, and she would get her kids back, and it wouldn't be like before. It is no secret I don't get along with the guy, so we start the fighting routine all over again, and one day, we just lost it on each other, and I decided it was time to move out. So this is the beginning, and at this point, she and Travis got into a fight because he was stupid enough to ask her if in the time they were separated, she had slept with someone else, and she said yes. He gets all mad and goes to the courthouse and files for divorce with her not working anymore. It was really a stressful time for my sister.

The person she had slept with was her coworker and grocery manager, and she was no longer seeing him. Her roommate, who she let move in, had no idea the two of them had been running around with each for months and was seeing him. So this guy who knew all her secrets—and she knew a lot of his—was still coming over all the time but seeing the roommate, and it would make Jenn so irritated and hurt, but she never told Justice.

One day I told her. I was so irritated seeing my sister hurt and sad over the situation. I explained it to Justice because the two of them had broken up over the Super Bowl. After telling Justice the whole story, instead of doing what a normal friend or person would do, which would be to stay away from him, she calls him and tries to work it out. She invites him back to the house with Jenn there and rubbed it in her face that the two of them had made up and had sex and that her bed was making all kinds of noise. Who in their right mind would do that to someone they consider a friend? That is no friend. That is a straight-up backstabbing bitch. Not to mention Jenn's kids fell in love with this guy, and they have to see the same guy over and hanging all over Justice and not giving two thoughts to Jenn or them anymore.

As this is going on with her, I swing over to Scott's house, mention the fact that I may be moving back to Fresno, and he hits me with, "We need to get together and file our divorce papers because I am moving and not sure what is going to happen with the bills and everything."

So with that, I am honestly like, "What are you talking about?" I have been trying this for years and told him, "Well, that's fine and all, but I don't have the money for it," and he says, "Yes, I know. I will talk care of it."

So my first thought was he is giving up on life. He doesn't want to do the blood sugar check anymore, or they found cancer had come back, and he doesn't want to fight. I let him go with his plan, and I am kind of sad because that's my friend, you know. He literally knows everything about me, and he has always been the person I can call and talk to about anything, and now I am going to lose that. So a couple of days go by, and I stop by, and he brings it up again. Says he got all the paperwork filled out and that he was ready to go to the courthouse. I said, "Okay, well, I am off tomorrow. Let's do it then."

So the day comes, and then I get the whole story from him. He met a girl from the Philippines on Facebook while playing Farmville, and he is running off to be with her. Now get this, she is the same age as his kids, and she has two babies of her own—one is four and the other two. So I am a little hurt by this. He didn't want to watch my baby or be with me, but he is running halfway across the world to be with this girl and raise her kids.

Apr. 2, 2015

So Phillip and I got a place together, which we move into at the end of April, and it was very selfish of me because I just wanted out of my sister's. I don't want to be with him. He is great with my baby, and he helps with him, but I don't love him, and I just think I am using him. I have told him this over and over, and I have stressed the fact that I think I am only with him for the baby and that it is not fair to him. Not to mention my son is getting attached, and his first word was "dada" as he was crawling over toward him.

I went to the bar the other day and was sitting there by myself just watching Ray work. He was not talking to me, but I saw that smile that I fell in love with the very first time that I had seen him those years earlier. As I drove home, which was an hour away, I thought about him all the way. Phillip is working, and so I texted him and said, "Sorry, this is not going to work. I am pretty sure I am still in love with Ray, and even though it's been months since we even talked or slept together, I still miss and care about him."

Phillip explains to me that he cares about me and Christopher and that Ray had lied and cheated and that I would be stupid to go back. However, if you think about it, I lied and cheated first, and I got pregnant. He was the bigger person and stayed by my side and gave me an escape outlet when everyone else I knew left me high and dry. Whether it was just for sex or not, he still had me over. Yeah, so he never asked about the baby or anything, but he still made me feel normal. When I had no one to talk to and no one to see, he was there. I think this is why I miss him so much. I can't even stay mad at him, and for some reason, which no one will tell me, I think Hollie is living with him. I don't know why, but I just have that feeling, but, of course, I ask him, and he won't tell me, and no one else will.

April 16 2015

Jenn and I went to my aunt and my grandma's house. My grandma starts talking about my brother Robert and saying he is the only person who did something with his life and how she is so proud of him for what he has done. *Really!*

He is an army recruiter, so he lies to young people every day, convinces them to sign up, and feeds them lies and fairy tales. Anyways, the rest of the aunts show up, and they are all, "Yeah, he is married to this other lady," and on and on, so when I got home, I looked at my sister and was all like, "Yeah right, are you joking?" Both of us were so angry. I was sitting in front of my computer, and I was all like, "Whatever, I make good money at Vons, have an associate degree in medicine. I have full benefits and raise a small child with no help. So I looked at my sister, and she mentioned she looked into being a medical assistant on the computer and was going to start in the spring when Travis was home or had a better idea of his work schedule. So I typed it into the computer and submitted my information. Within minutes, I got a couple of calls. I have an interview Monday with one school and one tomorrow at Kaplan College. Got off the phone and told my sister she should go with and we would check it out together.

Apr. 18, 2015

So today was the first day of school. LOL. We went to Kaplan College Saturday, and the lady was so nice and made a comment, "Okay, when would you like to start?"

Me, being the smart-ass that I am, said, "Okay, how about tomorrow?"

She looked at me and says, "Funny you say that because we have a class starting Monday."

So Jen and I signed up. Talk about jumping on the opportunity. I hope she sticks it out with me, and on the twenty-fourth, I have plans to visit my dad in San Diego. When we get back from that, I am moving into my own place. The tension here in the house with Jenn and Travis and Justice and her little boy toy is too much for me. Sister and I are fighting like all the time, and the last straw was when she claimed my son doesn't even know who I am because I am always working and so on. So I went and packed my stuff and picked the first apartment they had opened back at the same place I was before and, without even looking at the apartment, booked it, and we are moving.

Apr. 29, 2015

After we moved into the apartment, my friend and her boyfriend needed a place to stay for a month or two, so we moved them in, and then Renee's mom passed away, and she needed a place to crash, so I went from confused about my feelings toward him to having three other adults in the house, and then I signed up for school again, and then Phillip got mad at work and all quiet in April. So everything was going so quick that it was hard to keep track. I didn't want to move. I enjoyed the time with my sister, but with her ex-husband or whatever you want to call him back, I couldn't do it anymore. We had so much fun these last few months, and now it's gone.

So in the following months, my friend and her boyfriend, Adam, who is Hollie's brother, moved out, and so we moved Renee into the bedroom, and the baby was now in my room with Phillip. My feelings didn't change toward him, and I still cared for and missed Ray deeply. On my spare time, I would sneak off to the bar and sit there and drink just so I can see him. At this time, we were not talking, and I am sure he still hated me, and I still had a lot of anger toward him for what he did. I was now working two jobs and had school, and I was always so tired. Phillip finally got a job, and I quit the second one I had and was doing just school and Vons. I saw very little of my baby boy and my roommates. I started feeling that empty thought again, and so then the cutting started back up. I did okay hiding it for a little while and then started back at Chevron in August. With two jobs and school, I had no time—not for me, not for my baby, and not for any relationship that I thought I wanted. Then one day, I finally texted Ray, and I asked—more like, begged—for a second chance. I told him, "Why can't I have a second chance? I am sorry, and you give other people one. Why can't I have one?" To my surprise, he asked me to come over.

I was so scared and nervous, and I don't know why. This was the man I truly cared for, aside from my husband. This man stole my heart and cared for me while I was caring for someone else's child. This man stuck by me and didn't once tell my secret to anyone or judge me. This man, no matter what, always put a smile on my face when I was at my worse. However, this is the man who has broken me, made me cry, and made me cut. I was so scared to open my heart back up to him. For the first couple of weeks, it was only sex, and then I was gone. I didn't want to hang around because I didn't want my heart to want him. I didn't want to feel that hurt again. I didn't want to love him again, but in all reality, I was still in love with him. I started seeing Ray again in September, but then a few weeks later, my life would once again change, and this time, there was no way I could stop it, and there was nothing I could do without going against everything.

A couple of weeks after ending it completely with Phillip and starting back with Ray, I found out that once again I was pregnant with Philip's child because, yes, Ray is fixed, and the only person I was seeing at the time was Philip. With two jobs and school and just finally getting the man I cared about to give me a second chance, I was forced to make a stand. So after leaving Ray's house one night, I sent him a message and told him. A couple of days later, he texted me two or three times, and I didn't respond. How could I? My response to him was, "No, I am not seeing Phillip, but what do I do? I begged you for a second chance, and it was too late. I didn't know I was already pregnant. I am sorry for that." He wrote back something along the lines of "Yeah, it's not like you haven't done this before."

I hate to even say this on paper, but I was praying that when I went into that appointment, the doctor wouldn't find a heartbeat or that I would miscarry or lose the baby. As bad as that sounds, and I know I am probably going to hell for this, I didn't want to lose Ray again. I fought so hard for him to notice me, to give me a second chance, for him to know that I screwed up and that I was sorry, and I didn't want him to leave. I know he may never acknowledge the fact that I truly love him and want to be with him, and I will never know his feelings for me, but I don't want to live life without him.

Now let me go into the current situation with Phillip, and now this is going to take everything back for a minute. Now to understand Phillip and the whole picture, we're going to start from the top. See, when I meet him, he was yes a virgin. He lived at home with his mom. Not that money is everything or anything but paper, I asked Philip what did he spend all his money on. Anyone who made that kind of money and living with his mom and not having a family to support would have had a ton. So he tells me about his addiction I guess, you would call it that. So he has this little problem. He plays it off as being lonely, and for him to feel wanted, he would find these girls online. Now when I say "girls online," I am talking, like, hot girls, skinny little things some with fake boobs, some with really nice butts—whatever you name it. He would spend hours talking to them and listening to their sob story and eventually send them money for whatever reason. Some sent naked photos back, some did chat and videos, and some promised the fact that if he sent money, it would help them fix whatever problem they were having and come be with him. So before we got together, he had done this, and I was under the assumption that when we got together, he had stopped. I was the fool because he was still doing this, not as much, but still doing it.

The first doctor's appointment I had, I walked out to my car to find roses and a ring in my front seat and a note saying, "I am not asking you to marry me. Just know I will always be here for you and the kids." Aw, that was sweet. Right! Okay, so I get home, and he is still out doing whatever, and his computer is sitting on the chair, and it's open. I see a picture go by, and it's a naked girl. So out curiosity, I go look. I see this whole conversation and Skype messages to where they have called each other, and she was masturbating with toys so he can jack off and how much money she needed and so on, and this was the same morning he put a ring in my car. Are you serious? Not to mention the money he sent, and I just told him two weeks before that I was pregnant with his child, and he just sent $200 with the promise to send another $150 in two days when he got paid! Oh, talk about blood boiling, so I texted him told him to keep the ring or give it to her, that I was done and was so mad. Not to mention all the lies he told his mom about me. Mind you, she used to like me, and now she hates me. Her words were, "You're going to be with her? She is using you and sleeping around, and maybe you should look into the fact that she is not married anymore and not even with her son's dad anymore. What kind of person is she?" So this is why we are currently in separate bedrooms and not really talking—because he likes to lie about me to his family, my family, our friends, and anyone who would actually listen. He had even went as far as telling a coworker of ours that the only reason he feels he needs to stick around is because when we first got together, I gave him an STD. Wow, seriously, I yelled so loud at him that I think the apartment complex across the street heard me. I told him to leave, that I was done, and that I wasn't keeping this baby because I didn't want to deal with him, his mom, and his little girlfriends on the computer. So he tells me he was deleting all his friends that he had told lies to about me, and yes, I believed him.

So I played an evil, rude, just straight-up messed-up trick on him that was way out of character on my part. So back in June or July, one of the last times I caught him lying to me about his little girlfriends on the computer and we had called it off, I wanted to see if he was indeed telling me the truth, so I went playing on the computer, looking at pictures, and I found one—this cute blonde model from the UK. I downloaded a copy of the pictures and made a fake Facebook profile and a PayPal account for my new friend Samantha Jones. No, mind you, I don't remember her actual name. Then I find Phillip's account online and send him a friend request. This boy instantly accepts and starts right away. He is supposed to be at work.

He sent instant messages to Samantha and tells her she is so beautiful, and he starts asking questions like "Where you at," "What you doing," and "Maybe we can grab lunch or dinner." This continues for a couple days, and I said, "Okay, let's meet," so at this time, I am trying to find an address and figure out who is going to play this role for me. One, I don't know anyone who looks like that, and two, what address am I going to use? My friend from school says, "Use mine." I will tell him she is my cousin when he shows up. Okay, game on. So I get home from school, and Phillip feeds me this storyline about how he is going out for lunch with one of the boys and how he would ask if I wanted to go but knows I hate raw fish, so it's most likely not going to happen. This whole time, he is just lying to my face. This is the conversation between the two.

P: Or if you wanna meet up for dinner
S: that would be cool around wht time

P: Which Savemart did you work at if you don't mine
P: Or maybe drinks, I'm sure Brandon would come with Maybe sushi
S: o I don't know Brandon I wAS looking at his picture form your profile and accidenyly clicked send, sushi sounds great I can meet you around 8, my mom should be home by then and I went take her car

P: How but a little earlier, I can always come pick you up I know but Brandon is my friend

P: My roommate works overnights so I watch baby for her

S: why don't I come over when she goes to work or are you guys seeing each

P: We were at one point seeing each other

S: o what happened, is that not weird still living there

P: It's a two bedroom Lol

This is part of the conversation they had on September 27, 2015, so he clearly knows we're not together. It keeps going, but to save the man a little, I am not going to put the rest of the conversation here. The whole thing about this was, yes, I made the fake profile and, yes, I continue to act if I was Samantha, but he sent her a picture of my baby, some girl he doesn't know, and tried to tell me he has known her for years and that they used to go drinking together. He got mad at me for overreacting about the pictures of my baby going out to some people I don't know. Thank God it was a fake profile that I set up. I told him, "You don't know what was on the other end of that. It could have been some sick monster, and you just put my baby boy out there like that." He agrees it was wrong and he was lonely once again, and that's why he did it. I had to tell him, "Honestly, I couldn't care if you were on your deathbed. Out of all the sick people that are on the Internet, you don't send a picture of my baby to some random person."

Chapter 14

Jan. 27, 2016

Okay, so a couple days ago, I was at Chevron working. It was Friday and Sunny's birthday, so he got the day off. I am there with the two new owners, and Phillip is texting me, but I don't have time to write him back, and then I see a message that says, "Guess you don't want to be with me anymore or need me, so good-bye, I am out."

I texted him back, "What do you mean you're out, and when do you plan on leaving, and where is my son?" He has left my son alone before, and being a mom, I wanted to know were my kid was. He wouldn't text back; I got no response. I kept texting, tried calling him. I called my friends to see if they could go by my house and check on my son. No response from anyone, so, yes, I call the cops.

An hour and a half later, as I walk out of Chevron and drive like a crazy person to the apartment, I find out my baby is at my dad's house, and Phillip is gone. He doesn't come back till Monday, asking for forgiveness. When I'd gone to take a bath, I'd texted him and said, "Look, you said you didn't want to leave. Well, I am gone. I am moving out."

He wrote back and said, "I am on my way." He gets home and asks why I look sad. He thinks it's because of him.

"It's not. I am sad because out of the busy life I have, I now have to spend four more hours out of my day to drive and drop off or pick up my child. I lose four more hours that I can be spending with him taking him up to a babysitter."

He then has the balls to tell me, "Well, if you're that worried about it, the other day I came home on my lunch, and Christopher was up in his crib playing, and you were sound asleep." He says, "How do you think I feel when you leave the baby, who you claim to care about, in his crib till 9 o'clock?"

Okay, so with that, I am mad and hurt. "Do you really think I don't feel like a bad mother when I wake up, and it's nine or ten o'clock, and I am still in bed and Christopher is up? You don't think that makes me feel like awful? Makes me feel like I am a failure to my child? Yes, it does. I try and leave my door open so I can hear him while he is up or if he starts crying. I can't help the fact that between both of our work schedules, this one fits better. I don't have to pay to have him in day care, but ultimately, I get off late. Working twelve hours a day, taking care of an eighteen-month-old, and being five months pregnant, I am tired."

So he is sitting here begging for another chance. He says he was overwhelmed with Christopher and was afraid of what he would do to Christopher out of anger. Okay, because that is the last thing a mother wants to hear. I was so mad that he drove my son up to my dad's house—my dad just had major back surgery—and dropped him off.

He claimed, "Well, your dad said it was fine."

I told him, "What did you expect him to say? That is his grandson. Of course, he is going to say okay. He is not even supposed to lift more than five pounds, and you take a forty-pound child up there and drop him off because you needed a break? Well, I got news for you. As a parent, you don't get a break. You don't get to call it quits because you want the weekend off." I told him, "What the hell are you going to do with a two-year-old and a newborn? You can't just walk away and take a weekend to yourself. It doesn't work like that."

He then goes, "Well, I was under the impression we were trying to work it out."

I said, "*Wow*, what in the world gave you that impression? The fact that we have separate bedrooms, the fact that we don't talk, or the fact we have not slept together in over five months? Please tell me where you thought or how you thought we were trying to work anything out."

So with that in mind, yes, he and I still live together, but in separate rooms. He plans on staying and helping with his child as well as Christopher. I have finished and graduated school and currently looking for a job in the medical field. I can't simply end his, because it is a diary of my confused and broken soul. My journey will continue with or without help, but I have and will make better choices and decisions about my life and for my children. I went from hiding my feelings to openly expressing them with the world to better my life and to overcome many and painful obstacles that not only I have faced but my sister and family as well. This is only part of my story, and my story will continue. I will become a better person. I will live my life to the fullest and make the most of it.